Daniel March

Public Worship, Partly Responsive

Designed for any Christian congregation

Daniel March

Public Worship, Partly Responsive
Designed for any Christian congregation

ISBN/EAN: 9783337037710

Printed in Europe, USA, Canada, Australia, Japan

Cover: Foto ©Lupo / pixelio.de

More available books at **www.hansebooks.com**

PUBLIC WORSHIP.

Partly Responsive.

DESIGNED FOR ANY CHRISTIAN CONGREGATION.

With an Introduction,

BY

Rev. DANIEL MARCH, D. D.

PHILADELPHIA:
SMITH, ENGLISH & CO.,
710 ARCH STREET.
NEW YORK: A. D. F. RANDOLPH & CO.

PREFATORY NOTE.

THIS book contains complete services for the morning and afternoon (or evening) of five Sundays, and a service also for a sixth Sunday; which latter is abbreviated from the Episcopal Book of Common Prayer, and may be used at pleasure. The work has been prepared for use in college chapels, in schools, in Public Institutions, in Reformatory Houses, at sea-side and other resorts, in places where there is no settled ministry, and in short, wherever Christians desire to worship, — no clergyman being present, — and where a Responsive Service is desired, but where there is an unwillingness to use the Liturgy of the Episcopal Church.

It is not intended to be a complete *Church Manual;* therefore no forms for funerals or marriages, or for the administration of the Sacraments, have been supplied. The young pastor, however, more accustomed to the composition of sermons than prayers, may find some help from these forms, which, it is hoped, are not declamatory, or oratorical, or fine; not too familiar, tedious, or particular, didactic or sermonizing; but simple, dignified, and devotional.

"It cannot but appear strange that, when sermons are composed with so much care and pains, we should leave our prayers altogether to the impulse of the moment; as if it were more needful that our speeches to our fellow-men should be well ordered, than our addresses to God. In every point of view, extempore preaching is far more natural and becoming than extempore prayer; because any want of order, propriety, or solemnity, which is so difficult to be altogether avoided in unpremeditated speech, is far less offensive in a discourse to our fellow-mortals than in those solemn appeals which we present in their name and our own to the Father of our spirits."

PHILADELPHIA, September, 1873.

INTRODUCTION.

MEN ought always to pray. By the original constitution of our nature, by the course of divine Providence, by the command of divine revelation, necessity is laid upon all men, always and everywhere, to pray. It is only by resisting or perverting the most profound and sacred instinct of our humanity that any one ever restrains prayer, or fails to offer the daily sacrifice of thanksgiving and praise. The first utterance of the child is a cry to the parent for help. And all who live in the blessed and immortal childhood of truth and love will delight to ask the one infinite and eternal Father for every good and perfect gift.

We use our best language when we address the wise and mighty among men. How much more should we be careful to choose right words, and order our speech with thoughtfulness and discretion, when we approach the infinite and eternal King. We spend years of toil and study in the endeavor to master the most effective modes of speaking to men who are as frail and imperfect as ourselves. How much more earnestly should we labor to acquire the gift of speaking acceptably to God.

This book assumes that the sacred exercise of prayer and worship can be learned and improved by the diligent study and daily use of the best thoughts and the best language of the purest and most cultivated minds. It marks out a clear and simple order of Christian service, such as would be suitable for any Sabbath of the year and for any company of people. Pursuing the course prescribed in this book, reverently and thoughtfully, any person of common intelligence can conduct Christian worship with propriety and with profit to all that join with him.

These sacred forms of sound words have been wrought out from the deep and chastened experience of the purest and noblest of minds in many ages of Christian faith. They are worthy to be held fast in mind and heart by frequent repetition. Humble in confession, special in petition, exalted in praise, they express the wants, the desires, and the aspirations of all hearts. If in any place there should be no preaching of the gospel save the united and devout reading of this service with the appropriate selections from the Scriptures, all who joined heartily in such worship would have truthful and exalted views of God and duty, and they would know the way of salvation by Christ.

I have not been accustomed to the use of written formulas in conducting public worship. But I have felt the need of more order, fulness, and propriety than ordinarily appear in extemporaneous prayers from the pulpit. And I have desired some simple, familiar, and accepted form of worship in which minister and people alike can join with heart and voice. The preparation of this manual is a sign that many others have felt the same want, and it seems to me that the selections and the order of service set forth in the book are well fitted to answer an increasing demand. If the widely extended movement towards the adoption of some written and responsive form of worship can be made to follow the lead of this manual, it will be safely and wisely led. I feel assured that the work of the compiler will be accepted by many with full and hearty approbation; and that many others, who make no public use of prescribed forms in worship, will thank him for helping them to attain a richer, purer, and more scriptural expression of devotional feeling when speaking for themselves and others in prayer.

DANIEL MARCH.

CONTENTS

	PAGE
FIRST SUNDAY. — MORNING SERVICE	13
" " AFTERNOON SERVICE	21
SECOND SUNDAY. — MORNING SERVICE	27
" " AFTERNOON SERVICE	35
THIRD SUNDAY. — MORNING SERVICE	43
" " AFTERNOON SERVICE	52
FOURTH SUNDAY. — MORNING SERVICE	60
" " AFTERNOON SERVICE	68
FIFTH SUNDAY. — MORNING SERVICE	76
" " AFTERNOON SERVICE	85
SIXTH SUNDAY. — MORNING SERVICE	95
" " AFTERNOON SERVICE	114
PSALTER. — SELECTIONS FROM THE PSALMS	131
SELECTIONS FROM OTHER PARTS OF THE SCRIPTURES	198

Public Worship.

First Sunday.

MORNING SERVICE.

[*The congregation being assembled, the Minister may recite one or more of the following sentences.*]

SEEK ye the Lord while He may be found; call upon Him while He is near. Let the wicked forsake his way, and the unrighteous man his thoughts; and let him return unto the Lord, and He will have mercy upon him, and to our God, for He will abundantly pardon.

Let all the earth fear the Lord; let all the inhabitants of the world stand in awe of Him: for He spake, and it was done; He commanded, and it stood fast.

Blessed is the nation whose God is the Lord; and the people whom He hath chosen for His own inheritance.

Behold, the eye of the Lord is upon them that fear Him, upon them that hope in His mercy.

Having these promises, Brethren, let us draw near to the throne of grace with true hearts, in full assurance of faith. Let us pray.

FIRST PRAYER.

O God, whom heaven and the heaven of heavens cannot contain, but who dwellest with humble and contrite hearts, look in Thy mercy upon us who are here assembled, according to Thine ordinance, to offer up our sacrifices of prayer and praise before Thy divine majesty.

Grant unto us Thy Holy Spirit, we entreat Thee, O Lord, to guide and sanctify us, that we may be acceptable in Thy sight, and may obtain our petitions; for we come before Thee not in our own name, but in the name of our great High-Priest and Advocate, Jesus Christ.

[*At the end of this, and all the other prayers, the Congregation should answer,* Amen.]

We thank Thee, O God our heavenly Father, for that message of grace and mercy which Thou hast sent unto us in the gospel of thy Son Jesus Christ. Dispose and enable us, we pray Thee, to receive the same in faith and love, and to walk worthy of our high calling, not turning the grace of God into licentiousness, but bringing forth continually the fruits of holy obedience, to the praise of Thy name; through Jesus Christ our Lord, who taught us thus to pray:

Our Father which art in heaven, Hallowed be thy name. Thy kingdom come. Thy will be done in earth, as it is in heaven. Give us this day our daily bread. And forgive us our debts, as we forgive our debtors. And lead us not into temptation, but deliver us from evil. For thine is the kingdom, and the power, and the glory forever. *Amen.*

The Psalter for the day of the month. Lesson from Old Testament. Hymn.

SECOND PRAYER.

O God, who hast given Thy holy Word to be a light unto our feet and a lamp unto our path, guide our steps at all times in the way of Thy precepts. Suffer us not to go astray from Thee, or to err from Thy truth. Acknowledging our own ignorance and the deceitfulness of our hearts, we call upon Thee, O God, for help and deliverance, who savest all them that put their trust in Thee. *Amen.*

O Lord our merciful Father, be pleased to guide and defend us in all our ways, that we may be delivered in all dangers and temptations of this day; and may so follow the example and pattern which Thy dear Son hath left us, both in joyfully bearing and constantly performing Thy holy will, that we may glorify Thy name, and may abide in Thy love; even as He kept Thy commandments and abode in Thy love. *Amen.*

O Lord God Almighty, who makest all things work together for good to them that love Thee, we pray that Thou wouldst so order the course of Thy providence respecting us, and so enlighten and purify our souls, that all the events of this life may be made conducive to our eternal salvation; through Jesus Christ our Lord. *Amen.*

Almighty and most merciful Father, who workest in Thy children both to desire and to perform those things that please Thee, grant us grace that we may pursue our several callings and duties in the world with a devout, holy, and heavenly mind, considering that we are ever in Thy presence and under Thine eye; that in all our works and labors, working the work of God, and laboring for the meat that endureth unto everlasting life, we may be found good and faithful servants, and may finally enter into the joy of our Lord. *Amen.*

O God, everlasting and almighty, who art the Creator and Preserver of all men, and who willest not that any should perish, but that all should come to repentance, send forth Thy light and Thy truth among all nations. *Amen.*

Guide all Thy flock in the paths of truth, righteousness, and peace, and make them to be numbered with Thy saints in glory everlasting. *Amen.*

Comfort the afflicted; send consolation and joy to

those that are in trouble and sorrow; hear the groaning of the prisoners; deliver the oppressed from him that spoileth him; relieve the wants of the poor, and save the afflicted people. Arise, O God, for judgment, and save all the meek of the earth. *Amen.*

O God, who hast revealed to us the light of Thy gospel and called us into the fellowship of Thy Son, grant that we may put away all the works of darkness, and may walk in purity, uprightness, and truth; that we may have fellowship with Thee, for Thou art light, and in Thee there is no darkness at all; that so, when the shadows of this mortal life are passed away, we may behold those things which the eye of man hath not seen, and be made partakers of everlasting glory; through Christ our Lord. *Amen.*

Grant, we pray Thee, O Lord, that we, who have believed in the name of Thy Son Jesus Christ, may die daily through His death, and also may be quickened through the power of His resurrection. Being crucified with Christ, may we live to Thee through faith in the Son of God, who loved us and gave Himself for us; that when He shall appear in glory, we also may be manifested as Thy sons, and may inherit the kingdom which Thou hast prepared for them that love Thee. *Amen.*

Almighty and most gracious God, look in Thy compassion upon our manifold infirmities, and uphold us by Thy mighty power. Let us not faint or be weary in running the race that is set before us;

but, animated by Thy promises, may we be strong both to do and to endure Thy holy will, looking unto our merciful High-Priest, Jesus Christ, who Himself suffered and was tempted, and is able to succor us when we are tempted. *Amen.*

Almighty God, the Creator of all things, who hast so loved the world as to give Thy Son, that they who were far off might be brought near unto Thee, send forth Thy gospel into all lands, and hasten the time when all the kindreds of the nations shall turn unto the Lord, and Jew and Gentile shall be one flock, under one Shepherd, Jesus Christ. *Amen.*

O God, merciful Father, look upon all Thy family, which Thy Son Jesus Christ hath purchased with His own blood. Deliver them from ignorance and sin, and from the power of death; and grant them a portion in that kingdom, the hope of which Thou hast inspired in the hearts of Thy chosen; through Jesus Christ, who was dead and is alive again, and liveth for ever; and who sitteth at Thy right hand, till all things are put under His feet, and Death, the last enemy, is destroyed. *Amen.*

Send forth Thy Holy Spirit the Comforter, we entreat Thee, O Thou God of all grace and consolation, into the hearts of those who, under Thy wise and holy providence, are called to endure any sickness, trouble, or adversity. Let Thy fatherly chastisement, though for the present it be not joyous but grievous, work the peaceable fruit of righteousness in them that are exercised thereby. Enrich their souls with faith and hope, with patience and fortitude; and while they look at those things which are not seen, may their present affliction work for them a far more exceeding, even an eternal weight of glory. *Amen.*

We pray that Thou wouldst grant a spirit of wisdom and judgment to the Ministers and Counsellors of the States, to Magistrates, Judges, and all that are invested with authority; that we, under them, may lead a quiet and peaceable life in godliness and honesty, adorning the doctrine of God our Saviour. *Amen.*

And bestow Thy blessing upon all conditions of men among us. Bless them in the work of their hands; prosper their honest industry; grant unto them the things that are needful for the body and the life that now is; above all, make them rich towards God and heirs of thine everlasting kingdom. *Amen.*

We pray for our kindred, our friends, and all whom Thou hast made the instruments of Thy grace and bounty to us, that Thou wouldst reward and bless them abundantly; and also for our enemies, that Thou wouldst grant them repentance, and enable us to forgive them from the heart. *Amen.*

O God, whose blessing is upon them that fear Thee from generation to generation, we desire to commit ourselves to Thee as a faithful Creator, who hast said, "I will never leave thee nor forsake thee." Strengthen us that we may seek first Thy kingdom and righteousness, trusting in Thy promise that all things needful shall be added unto us. And seeing we brought nothing into this world and can take nothing out, may we, having food and raiment, be therewith content. *Amen.*

Lesson from New Testament. Hymn. Sermon

PRAYER.

Almighty, Eternal God, who dost so heartily desire our salvation, and dost so faithfully warn us in manifold ways to think in earnest on the things that belong to our peace; we pray Thee humbly give us Thy good Spirit, that we may believe in this Thy great love and faithfulness with our whole hearts, and may not trifle away our time of grace, but follow Thy voice which bids us come to Thee while it is yet to-day; for the sake of Thy dear Son Jesus Christ our Lord. *Amen.*

Hymn. Doxology. Benediction.

First Sunday.

AFTERNOON SERVICE.

[*The congregation being assembled, the Minister may recite one or more of the following sentences.*]

LOOK unto me and be ye saved, all the ends of the earth; for I am God, and there is none else.

The Lord is nigh unto them that call upon Him; to all that call upon Him in truth.

He will fulfil the desire of them that fear Him: He also will hear their cry, and will save them.

The Lord reigneth; let the people tremble: He sitteth between the cherubim; let the earth be moved.

The Lord is great in Zion; and He is high above all the people.

Exalt ye the Lord our God, and worship at His footstool; for He is holy.

Brethren, let us with humble and contrite hearts draw near to the throne of grace, in the name of our great High-Priest and Advocate, Jesus Christ.

FIRST PRAYER.

O Lord our heavenly Father, who hast commanded us not to forsake the assembling of ourselves together, be pleased to sanctify and bless our meeting together at this time; and grant that, by Thy Word and Spirit, our minds may be enlightened, our hearts cleansed, and our wills directed to keep Thy holy commandments; through Jesus Christ our Redeemer. *Amen.*

We confess our sins before Thee, O God, Thou righteous Judge, to whom all things are naked and open. We have done evil in Thy sight, transgressing Thy law, which is holy, just, and good; and we are verily guilty before Thee.

We praise Thy name that when we were enemies we were reconciled unto Thee by the death of Thy Son, and for the comfortable assurance that if we confess our sins, Thou art faithful and just to forgive us our sins, and to cleanse us from all unrighteousness.

Be it unto us, O Lord, according to Thy word.

Justify us freely by Thy grace, through the redemption that is in Christ Jesus; that, having our hearts sprinkled from an evil conscience, we may serve Thee in holiness and righteousness all our days, rejoicing in the hope of Thy glory, and waiting for the appearing and kingdom of our Lord and Saviour Jesus Christ. *Amen.*

O God, Thou Father of lights, and fountain of all wisdom and knowledge, we thank Thee that Thou hast sent Thy Son Jesus Christ into the world to enlighten our darkness, and to guide us in the ways of truth and righteousness. May we hear His voice; may we know and embrace the doctrine which He hath taught us; may we render a willing obedience to His precepts; may we follow His example; and, finally, may we receive those exceeding great and precious promises which He hath given us. Grant this, we beseech Thee, O Lord, through the same Jesus Christ, who is our Prophet, our Priest, and our King. *Amen.*

Psalter for the day. Lesson from Scriptures. Hymn.

SECOND PRAYER.

O God, whose word is quick and powerful and sharper than a two-edged sword, grant unto us who are here before Thee, and to all Thy people everywhere, that we may receive Thy truth into our hearts in faith and love. By it may we be taught and guided, upheld and comforted; that we be no longer children in understanding, but grow in grace unto the stature of a perfect man in Christ Jesus, and so be prepared for every good word and work, to the honor of Thy name; through Jesus Christ our Lord. *Amen.*

Be pleased, almighty and most gracious God, to increase our faith, hope, and charity, our patience, fortitude, and meekness, our zeal and diligence in Thy service. May we, through Thy grace, mortify all sinful affections, resist and subdue all evil habits, and abound in every good work. Let our good resolutions be ripened into acts and habits of holiness and virtue, that we may be as epistles of Christ, Thy laws being written in our hearts and upon our whole lives; that so we may walk worthy of our high vocation and adorn the doctrine of God our Saviour. *Amen.*

Dwell in our hearts, we pray Thee, O Lord God, and make us temples of Thy Holy Spirit; that whereas in ourselves we are weak, corrupt, and mortal, we may through Thee be strengthened and sanctified, and finally, having obtained the victory over death, may reign in immortal life; through Him who died for our sins and rose again for our justification, and liveth and reigneth with Thee the Father in the unity of the Spirit, world without end. *Amen.*

Gracious God, Father of mercies, who hast sent Thy Son into the world, that whosoever followeth Him might not walk in darkness, grant, we beseech Thee, that Thy gospel may speedily be preached among all nations, that all flesh may see the salvation of God.

Let the kingdoms of this world at length become the kingdoms of our Lord and of His Christ. Take the veil from the heart of the Jew, that he may see the end of that law which was commanded unto the fathers, and let all the nations turn unto the Lord; through our Mediator Jesus Christ. *Amen.*

O God, everlasting and almighty, whose grace hath appeared, bringing salvation to all men, teach us to deny ungodliness and worldly lusts, and to live soberly, righteously, and godly in this present world, looking for the blessed hope, even the glorious appearing of the great God and our Saviour Jesus Christ, who gave Himself for us that He might redeem us from all iniquity. *Amen.*

Eternal God, who quickeneth all things, and by whose Spirit the Church, which is the body of Thy Son, is governed and sanctified, we pray that all who profess His religion may adorn His doctrine by walking as Christ walked, that they and we may at length obtain that incorruptible crown which Thou hast promised to them that love Thee.

And we beseech Thee, O Lord, who hast built Thy Church upon the foundation of the apostles and prophets, Jesus Christ Himself being the chief corner-stone, to grant a spirit of wisdom and power to Thy servants who are appointed to labor in the ministry of the Word; that by their doctrine and example Thy saints may be built up in their holy faith, and sinners may be converted unto Thee. And everywhere let Thy word have free course and be glorified; through Him who is the Apostle and High-Priest of our profession, Jesus Christ. *Amen.*

Father of mercies, look down in compassion upon the sick and afflicted, upon the poor, the miserable, and the dying, upon the friendless, the despairing, and the tempted, and upon all who are in danger, necessity, or tribulation.

Send them comfort and deliverance, O God; and

do Thou, who makest all things work together for good to them that love thee, sanctify their pains and sorrows to the health and salvation of their souls in the day of our Lord Jesus Christ. *Amen.*

We beseech Thee, O God, to bless all men; bring them to the knowledge and obedience of the truth.

Break Thou the arm of the oppressor everywhere; and scatter the people that delight in war;

And in all the earth let Thy kingdom come, which is righteousness and peace and joy in the Holy Ghost.
Amen.

Hymn. Sermon.

PRAYER.

O Lord, have mercy upon us; grant that we may receive Thy word into good and honest hearts, and may bring forth the fruit of good living, to the honor of Thy great name. *Amen.*

O God, who hast given the day to man for labor, and the night for rest, protect us by Thy watchful providence during the coming night, and all the nights and days of our pilgrimage. Cover all our sins with Thy mercy, as Thou coverest the earth with darkness during the night-watches. And when our days are ended, and our work is finished in this world, may we depart hence in the blessed assurance of Thy favor, and in the certain hope of the resurrection to immortal life, which Thou hast given us in our Lord and Saviour Jesus Christ. *Amen.*

Hymn. Doxology. Benediction.

Second Sunday.

MORNING SERVICE.

[*The congregation being assembled, the Minister may recite the following sentences.*]

DRAW nigh unto God, and He will draw nigh unto you.

Cast away from you all your transgressions, whereby ye have transgressed; and make you a new heart and a right spirit: for why will ye die, O house of Israel? For I have no pleasure in the death of him that dieth, saith the Lord God: wherefore turn yourselves, and live ye.

Brethren, we are here assembled in obedience to the command that we forsake not the assembling of ourselves together, and in hope of that promise which our Lord Jesus Christ hath given to His disciples, that wherever two or three shall meet together in His name, He will be in the midst of them. Let us, therefore, with reverence and godly fear, draw nigh to the throne of grace, that we may obtain mercy and find grace to help in time of need.

FIRST PRAYER.

Almighty God, the Maker of all things visible and invisible, the Creator and Preserver, who hast sent Thy Son to bring us near, who by our sins were far off, and to redeem us, and make us sons of God, and heirs of eternal life; grant unto us Thy grace and blessing, as we are here assembled to offer up our common supplications before Thy Divine Majesty; to confess our sins and iniquities, and to render thanks unto Thy name for Thy great goodness and mercy.

May we put away all heedlessness and levity, all vain thoughts and distracting cares; and may we draw near to Thy presence with earnest, humble, and faithful hearts, in the Spirit of holiness and truth.

And let our worship and service, being offered in the name and Spirit of Thy Son, be acceptable to Thee, and profitable to us; through Him who is our Mediator and Advocate, Jesus Christ. *Amen.*

We confess before Thee, O God, our Heavenly Father, that we are miserable sinners; for we have transgressed thy holy laws times innumerable in thought, word, and deed.

We have not loved Thee with all our hearts; neither have we loved our neighbor as ourselves.

We have not glorified Thee with our bodies and our spirits; but we have lived in ungodliness, in pride, and vanity; in envy and uncharitableness; in covetousness and discontent.

We have loved the world, and the things that are of the world, and have not set our affection on things above, or laid up treasure in heaven, where Christ, our risen Lord, sitteth at Thy right hand.

Almighty God, Father of our Lord Jesus Christ, who hast in Thy gospel proclaimed remission of sins to all them that believe in the name of Thy Son, and repent of their transgressions against Thee, confirm us, we beseech Thee, in the faith and hope of this Thy promise; and for this end so work in us by Thy Holy Spirit, that we may embrace and hold fast Thy truth in a pure conscience unto the end, and also may bring forth fruits meet for repentance; that being justified freely by Thy grace, and walking continually in the way of Thy commandments, we may glorify Thy holy name, and may know that we are indeed Thy children, and heirs of the kingdom which Thou hast promised to them that love Thee. *Amen.*

Our Father which art in heaven, Hallowed be Thy name. Thy kingdom come. Thy will be done in earth, as it is in heaven. Give us this day our daily bread. And forgive us our debts, as we forgive our debtors. And lead us not into temptation, but deliver us from evil: for Thine is the kingdom, and the power, and the glory, forever. *Amen.*

Psalter for the day. Old Testament Lesson. Hymn.

SECOND PRAYER.

O God, who desirest not sacrifice, and hast no delight in burnt-offering, but hast showed us what is good, and requirest of us to do justly, to love mercy, and to walk humbly with Thee, grant us, we pray Thee, true repentance of our sins and godly sorrow, and so direct and govern our hearts and lives that we may render a constant and unfeigned obedience to Thy holy laws; that, offering to Thee the sacrifices of righteousness, we may be acceptable in Thy sight, and may obtain our petitions; through Jesus Christ, who is our High-Priest and sacrifice. *Amen.*

O God, Thou King eternal, immortal, invisible, the blessed and only Potentate, may we, who cannot see Thee with the eye of flesh, behold Thee steadfastly with the eye of faith, that we faint not under the manifold temptations and afflictions of this mortal life, but endure as seeing Thee who art invisible; that after we have done and suffered Thy will upon the earth, we may behold the vision of God in heaven, and be made partakers of those joys unspeakable which Thou hast promised to them that love Thee. *Amen.*

O God, our bountiful Benefactor, we thank Thee for the bread that perisheth, and for all the good things of this present life. May we receive them with gratitude, and enjoy them with temperance and charity. But man liveth not by bread alone. Make us to hunger and thirst after righteousness; that our souls may at length be satisfied with the fulness of Thy truth and grace; through Him who is the bread of life and giveth life unto the world, Jesus Christ our Lord. *Amen.*

Most gracious God, who didst send Thy Son into the world to die for our sins, and to rise again for our justification; grant that we, who have been baptized into His death, may put away all the corruptions and pollutions of the old man; all evil thoughts, unholy desires, and malignant passions; and may we rise with Christ to newness of life; abounding in godliness, justice, charity, and meekness; in purity and temperance; in fortitude, patience, and resignation; that we may be indeed followers of Christ in all the steps of His blessed and holy life; and may walk worthy of our high vocation; through Him who is our Redeemer and Lord, and who suffered for us in the flesh, leaving us an example that we should follow His steps. *Amen.*

God of all grace and consolation, whose Son Jesus Christ hath ascended on high, leading captivity captive and receiving gifts for men, leave not us Thy family comfortless, but send forth into our hearts Thy Holy Spirit to abide with us forever; that we, being taught and quickened, purified and strengthened, by Thy heavenly grace, may faithfully and joyfully serve Thee all our days; through Christ our Lord. *Amen.*

Blessed Lord, whose will it is that all men should be saved, and who hast commanded us to make intercessions and prayers for all men, we offer up before Thee our supplications for the whole human race, that they may be brought to the knowledge and obedience of the truth:

For all Thy people upon earth, that they may fight the good fight and lay hold on eternal life; and may so run the race that is set before them that in due time they may obtain the prize:

For all the afflicted, that it may please Thee to sanctify, uphold, and comfort them, and to redeem their souls from all evil.

Look down from the height of Thy sanctuary, O merciful Father, upon the sick, the sorrowful, and the dying; upon widows and orphans; upon the despairing and the tempted; and upon those who have not God in all their thoughts. Lord, have mercy upon them, and upon us also, for we are men of like passions, and compassed about with infirmity. Grant unto us to be humble, sober, and watchful, that we may stand in the evil day.

We pray for our kindred, friends, and benefactors, that Thou wouldst enrich them with Thy favor, and grant unto them a portion in Thy heavenly kingdom:

And for our enemies; that Thou wouldst forgive them, and enable us to forgive them from the heart; that, rendering good for evil, we may be indeed Thy children, and perfect as our Father in heaven is perfect. *Amen.*

O God, thou King of glory, who rulest all the nations of the world, and to whom pertain all might, majesty, and dominion in heaven and earth, we beseech Thee to regard with Thy favor the President of the United States, the Governor of this commonwealth, the Members of both Houses of Congress, all Magistrates and Judges, and all persons invested with authority. Be pleased to grant unto them a spirit of wisdom and of the fear of the Lord; and may we, and all under them, lead a quiet and peaceable life in godliness and honesty, showing forth Thy praise, who hast called us out of darkness into the marvellous light of Thy gospel. *Amen.*

O God, by whose gracious providence we enjoy the good things of this present life, and also all things pertaining to godliness and the life eternal, we, Thy unworthy servants, unite with one heart in rendering thanks and praise unto Thy great name.

Enable us, we entreat Thee, O Lord, to manifest our gratitude by a willing and constant obedience to Thy righteous commands, and by walking, at all times, after the example of Him whom Thou didst send into the world to take away its sin, and make us sons of God, and heirs of immortal life; and who hath taught us, in the spirit of adoption, thus to pray:

Our Father which art in heaven, Hallowed be Thy name. Thy kingdom come. Thy will be done in earth, as it is in heaven. Give us this day our daily bread. And forgive us our debts, as we forgive our debtors. And lead us not into temptation, but deliver us from evil: For Thine is the kingdom, and the power, and the glory, forever. *Amen.*

Lesson from New Testament. Hymn. Sermon.

PRAYER.

Almighty and Eternal God, who hast graciously bestowed on us the clear light of Thy Word, whereby we, notwithstanding our sins, can attain through Christ a childlike trust in Thee; we humbly pray Thee give us Thy Holy Spirit, that we may trust Thy Word with our whole hearts, and, relying wholly upon Thee, may deny the world and ourselves, and bear the Cross after Thy dear Son in steadfast patience, through the same Jesus Christ our Lord. *Amen.*

Hymn. Doxology. Benediction.

Second Sunday.

AFTERNOON SERVICE.

[*The congregation being assembled, the Minister may recite the following sentences.*]

THE eyes of the Lord are upon the righteous; and His ears are open to their cry.

The Lord is nigh unto them that are of a broken heart; and saveth such as be of a contrite spirit.

Ask, and it shall be given you; seek, and ye shall find; knock, and it shall be opened unto you: for every one that asketh receiveth; and he that seeketh findeth; and to him that knocketh it shall be opened.

Brethren, let us draw near to the throne of grace with reverence and godly fear, in the name of our Lord and Saviour Jesus Christ. Let us pray.

FIRST PRAYER.

Almighty and everlasting God, who hast promised that in all places where Thou dost record Thy name Thou wilt meet with Thy servants and bless them, fulfil to us at this time Thy promise, we beseech Thee, and make us joyful in Thy house of prayer.

Solemnize and purify our minds: raise our hearts to Thee: endow us with wisdom and understanding: may we know, believe, and love Thy truth; and let the words of our mouths and the meditations of our hearts be acceptable in Thy sight, O Lord, our strength and our Redeemer. *Amen.*

Lord, have mercy upon us; for we daily sin against Thee, transgressing Thy holy laws, failing of the duty Thou requirest of us, and grieving Thy Spirit of grace. Through Jesus Christ Thy Son, who is the propitiation for our sins, and who ever liveth in Thy presence in heaven, our High-Priest and Mediator, be pleased, O Lord, merciful Father, to blot out all our offences, our ignorances and negligences, our unfaithfulness in Thy service, our sloth and pride, our love of the world, and all our secret faults and presumptuous sins, by which we have been disobedient unto Thy heavenly calling, and have merited Thy just displeasure. If Thou shouldst enter into judgment, we could not stand; but there is mercy with Thee that Thou mayest be feared.

O God, who despisest not the sighing of a contrite heart nor the desire of such as be sorrowful, grant unto us true repentance and godly reformation of life; that, being redeemed from our sins and vanities, we may henceforth walk in the way of Thy precepts in all things, and abound in good works; that so we may adorn the doctrine of God our Saviour, and make our calling and election sure. *Amen.*

O Lord our heavenly Father, who hast made Thy Son Christ to be wisdom and righteousness, sanctification and redemption to them that follow Him and obey His voice, vouchsafe unto us Thy Holy Spirit, we beseech Thee; that we may be wise unto salvation; may be just, upright, sincere, doing unto others as we would they should do unto us; may be purified from all base, unholy, and malignant passions; may be liberated and made free from bondage to the world, the flesh, and the devil; and finally may obtain the adoption, even the redemption of our bodies, that death may be swallowed up of victory. And these things we ask in His name who is the author and finisher of the faith, Jesus Christ our Saviour. *Amen.*

Psalter for the day. Lesson from Scripture. Hymn.

SECOND PRAYER.

O God, who didst speak in times past unto the fathers by the prophets, and hast, in these last days, spoken unto us by Thy Son, give us, we pray Thee, humble, teachable, and obedient hearts, that we may lend a willing ear to the doctrine which He hath taught us, and may embrace the same and hold it fast, to Thy honor and praise. *Amen.*

Deliver us, O Lord, from the instruction that causeth to err. Let not us receive for doctrines the commandments of men; seeing one is our Master, even

Christ, and all we are brethren. May we know the truth, and so be made free from all darkness and unbelief, from all error and sin. *Amen.*

And for this end give us, O Lord, the love of the truth; purify our souls from heedlessness and vanity, from hypocrisy and hardness of heart, from covetousness and love of the world, and from fleshly lusts which war against the soul; and endow us with seriousness and earnestness of spirit, that we may fight the good fight of faith, and lay hold of eternal life.

Amen.

Blessed Lord, who hath sent forth Thy Son Jesus Christ to die for our sins, and also, by His heavenly doctrine and holy life, to lead us in the paths of truth and righteousness, grant us Thy Holy Spirit to dwell in our hearts, to guide our lives, and to sanctify us wholly in spirit, soul, and body; that having glorified Thee upon the earth and finished the work Thou hast given us to do, we may obtain the victory over all our enemies, and reign in immortal life; through Him who is Thy Word made flesh, Jesus Christ. *Amen.*

O Thou great Master and Lord, who art calling us to serve Thee that we may be free, and art intrusting Thy talents to our keeping for a season, grant us mercy to be wise and faithful stewards even in that which is least. May we not abuse or bury Thy gift, but improve it to Thy glory; that when the Lord shall reckon with us, we may be found of Him in peace, and may enter into the joy of our Lord. *Amen.*

O God, who hast given us the promise of Thy heavenly rest, may we labor earnestly to enter into it. For this end quicken, we pray Thee, our faith and hope. Teach us to mortify whatever in us is earthly, carnal, and corrupt. Putting off the works of darkness, which cannot abide the light of Thy countenance, may we be clothed with truth, righteousness, and purity, and walk as Christ walked; that we may have confidence, and not be ashamed before Him at His coming. *Amen.*

Almighty and most merciful God, Father of lights and Fountain of all goodness, who didst send forth Thy Son to be the light of the world, that whoso followeth Him should not walk in darkness, be pleased so to illuminate and guide all pastors and teachers that they may fully know and faithfully declare Thy holy gospel; that the whole body of the Church may grow in faith and charity and patience, and may abound in every good word and work. *Amen.*

And we humbly entreat Thee, most merciful God, to receive graciously the sacrifices of praise and prayer which Thy people have this day throughout the world offered unto Thee. *Amen.*

Let the cry of Thy family enter into Thine ears, O Father; and send unto Thy children an answer in peace; through our Elder Brother Jesus Christ, who is also our High-Priest and Sacrifice. *Amen.*

O Lord, who art from everlasting to everlasting, who knowest the end from the beginning, and who hast given to Thy Son the heathen for His inheritance, hasten, we entreat Thee, the coming and kingdom of Thy Christ. *Amen.*

Let all the ends of the earth remember and turn to the Lord; let all the kindreds of the nations worship before Thee. And do Thou, who holdest the hearts of all men in Thy hand, open a great door and effectual for the preaching of Thy servants everywhere, that their sound may go into all the earth, and their words to the ends of the world. *Amen.*

O Lord, who art very pitiful and of tender mercy, who art the Father of the fatherless and the husband of the widow, and dost not willingly afflict or grieve the children of men, we who are ourselves in the body, lift up our hearts unto Thee on behalf of all our brethren who are in any affliction or distress.

Look down from Thy holy habitation upon the poor and destitute; upon the bereaved and the sorrowful, the sick and the dying; upon those that are in pain and anguish; upon such as are unjustly held in bondage; and upon all that are desolate and oppressed. *Amen.*

Send them speedy help and deliverance, O Thou Judge of the earth: and so enrich the souls of Thy afflicted servants with patience and hope, that their present trouble may conduce to their eternal salvation: and may they and we receive, in due time, the end of our faith; through our merciful High-Priest Jesus Christ, who suffered and was tempted, and is able to succor us when we are tempted. *Amen.*

Lord of all power and might, we call upon Thee whose mercies are from everlasting. We are ignorant, weak, and perverse: leave us not, O God, neither forsake us. Guide us with Thy counsel: uphold us by Thy power. Suffer us not to go astray from Thy ways: let us not be weary in well-doing. May we live in Thy fear all the days of our life; may we die in Thy favor; and let our portion be among Thy saints at the second and glorious appearing of our Lord and Saviour Jesus Christ. *Amen.*

Hymn. Sermon.

PRAYER.

O God our heavenly Father, suffer not the good seed of Thy Word to be caught away by the wicked one out of our hearts: neither let it be scorched of tribulation or persecution; or be choked with cares and pleasures of this life: but being received into good and honest hearts, may it bring forth abundantly, in us and in all Christians, the fruits of faith and good works, to the glory of Thy grace. *Amen.*

O Lord God, in whose presence there is no darkness, for thou dwellest forever in unapproachable light, keep and defend us and all Thy saints, in soul and body, during the coming night, and in all the darkness of this mortal life. *Amen.*

May we rest in the assurance of Thy favor; in the peace of a good conscience; in the hope of a better life; in the faith of Thy providence and protection; and in the love of Thy Spirit. *Amen.*

May we rise up again to diligence in our several callings, to work the work of God while the day lasts, seeing the night cometh in which no man can work. And whether we wake or sleep, may we live together with Christ. *Amen.*

Lighten our darkness, we beseech Thee, O Lord; and by Thy great mercy defend us from all perils and dangers of this night; for the love of Thy only Son, our Saviour, Jesus Christ. *Amen.*

Hymn. Doxology. Benediction.

Third Sunday.

MORNING SERVICE.

[*The congregation being assembled, the Minister may recite one or more of the following sentences.*]

O GIVE thanks unto the Lord; call upon His name; make known His deeds among the people. Sing unto Him; sing psalms unto Him; talk ye of all His wondrous works. Glory ye in His holy name; and let the hearts of them rejoice that seek the Lord.

There is no difference between the Jew and the Greek; for the same Lord over all is rich in mercy to all them that call upon Him. For whosoever shall call upon the name of the Lord shall be saved.

Brethren, seeing that we have a great High-Priest that is passed into the heavens, Jesus the Son of God, let us come boldly unto the throne of grace, that we may obtain mercy and find grace to help in time of need. Let us pray.

FIRST PRAYER.

O God, who art greatly to be feared in the assembly of Thy saints, accept, we entreat Thee, our sacrifices of praise and prayer: and though we are not worthy to approach Thy presence, or to ask anything of Thee, do Thou receive us graciously, and answer us; through our great High-Priest and Advocate Jesus Christ.

Amen.

Almighty God, we render thanks unto Thy great name that we have been preserved to see another of the days of the Son of man upon earth. For the sun and the shining light; for the succession of night and day, and summer and winter, and seed-time and harvest, and the ordinances of heaven; for Thy fatherly care and goodness to us the children of men; for Thy watchful providence and unspeakable mercy, we magnify Thy name, O God.

Thou art worthy, O Lord, to receive glory and honor and blessing; for Thou hast created all things, and Thou dost sustain them by Thy power; and when sin had disturbed the order and repose of Thy works, and caused the whole creation to groan and travail in pain, Thou didst send Thy Son to redeem it from the bondage of corruption, and to make peace by the blood of His cross; whereby He hath reconciled all things in heaven and earth.

O God, Maker and Governor of the world, who on the seventh day didst rest from all Thy works, and hast promised an everlasting rest to all Thy faithful servants, make us to rest from our works, as Thou didst from Thine; that we who are weary with our vanities, and heavy-laden with our sins and sorrows, may take up the yoke and burden of Jesus Christ, and so find rest unto our souls, for His yoke is easy and His burden is light. *Amen.*

We confess that we are miserable sinners before thee, O God; for we have transgressed Thy holy laws, and done despite to Thy good Spirit, and walked in counsels of our own.

Forgive us, O Lord God.

O Lord, we acknowledge that we have not loved Thee with all our heart, or believed Thy faithful Word, or hoped for Thy promises, but have been disobedient and rebellious.

Forgive us, O Lord God.

We have debased our souls with vain and earthly passions, setting our affection on things below, loving the world and laying up treasure upon earth; so that the love of the Father hath not been in us.

Neither have we been sober and watchful, nor mortified the deeds of the body: but our hearts have been overcharged with cares and pleasures of this life; and we have been conformed to the world.

Our own hearts condemn us, and Thou art greater than our hearts, and knowest all things.

Forgive us, O Lord, we beseech Thee.

<small>Psalter for the day. Lesson from Old Testament. Hymn.</small>

PRAYER.

Almighty God, Father of mercies, we render thanks and praise unto Thee for sending Thy Son into the world, that He might redeem us from our sins and miseries, and make us heirs, according to the hope of everlasting life.

Being justified by faith, may we have peace with Thee, through our Lord Jesus Christ: and grant us Thy grace, we beseech Thee, O Lord, that we may depart from all iniquity, and may be a peculiar people, zealous of good works, showing forth Thy praise, who hast called us out of darkness into Thy marvellous light. *Amen.*

God of all grace, be pleased to receive our prayer, through Thy well-beloved Son, who commanded us in the spirit of adoption thus to say:

Our Father which art in heaven, Hallowed be Thy name. Thy kingdom come. Thy will be done in earth, as it is in heaven. Give us this day our daily bread. And forgive us our debts, as we forgive our debtors. And lead us not into temptation, but deliver us from evil: For Thine is the kingdom, and the power, and the glory, forever. *Amen.*

O God, who in the beginning didst cause the light to shine out of darkness, and hast made Thy sun to rise again upon the world, scattering all the shades of night, shine in our hearts, we pray Thee, and deliver us from ignorance and error, from doubt and fear;

and so cleanse us by Thy Holy Spirit, that we, renouncing the hidden things of dishonesty, and all the unfruitful works of darkness, may walk before Thee in sincerity, purity, and righteousness; that we may have fellowship with Thee, and may be followers of Him whom Thou didst send to be the light of the world, Jesus Christ our Lord. *Amen.*

Almighty and most merciful God, who didst feed Thy people of old with manna in the wilderness, teaching us that man liveth not by bread alone, we thank Thee for the supply of our daily wants, for the bounties of Thy good providence, for life, and breath, and all things:

Especially for Jesus Christ, Thine unspeakable gift, who is the bread of God, coming down from heaven, and giving life unto the world. May we eat of this bread, and live forever. *Amen.*

Guide and strengthen us, O God, with Thy truth; refresh our fainting souls with Thy promises; animate our hearts, and purify them with Thy love; that we may walk with constancy in the way of Thy precepts: and having finished our earthly pilgrimage in faith and patience, may we at length be delivered from the toils and dangers of the wilderness, and enjoy forever Thy heavenly rest; through Him who is the author and finisher of the faith, Jesus Christ our Lord. *Amen.*

O God, omnipotent and everlasting, who art the Saviour of all men, specially of them that believe, and whose eternal providence is over all Thy works, so that a sparrow falleth not on the ground without Thee, and even the hairs of our head are numbered, we beseech Thee to help and deliver us, Thy servants, in all time of our trouble and adversity, and also in all time of our prosperity; that we be not overwhelmed with despondency and fear, or lifted up with presumption and pride; but enjoying Thy bounties with humility and thankfulness, and bearing Thy chastening with faith and hope, we may endure unto the end, and having finished the work Thou hast given us to do, may through Thy mercy enter into the joy of our Lord. *Amen.*

O eternal God, who didst speak unto Thine ancient Israel, out of the midst of thick darkness, with thunderings and lightnings and terrible majesty, we bless Thee that Thy grace and truth are now revealed unto us by Jesus Christ Thy Son; whom Thou hast sent forth, in the fulness of time, to redeem us; that we might no more be servants, in bondage under the elements of the world, but might be sons and heirs of God, through Him.

Send forth into our hearts, we entreat Thee, O Lord, the spirit of Thy Son. Inspire us with perfect love, which casteth out fear; that we may draw nigh to Thy throne of grace, at all times, with true hearts in full assurance of faith; and having served Thee in peace and joy all the days of our life upon earth, may at length be made partakers of Thy heavenly inheritance; through our great High-Priest, who is passed into the heavens, Jesus the Son of God. *Amen.*

Grant unto us grace, we beseech Thee, Almighty God, that as Thou hast taught us Thy will, so we may at all times choose and obey Thy holy laws; making our light shine before men, to the glory of Thy name; through Jesus Christ our Lord. *Amen.*

Almighty God, who hast made of one blood all nations, and whose will it is that all men should come to the knowledge of the truth and be saved, send forth the light of Thy gospel into all lands, and pour out Thy Spirit upon all flesh; that Thy name may be hallowed everywhere, and Thy kingdom may come, which is righteousness, peace, and joy in the Holy Ghost.

Take the veil from the heart of the Jew, that he may see the end of that which was commanded to his fathers: and let all the kindreds of the nations turn unto the Lord; through Him who hath broken down the partition between Jew and Gentile, and hath reconciled both unto Thee. *Amen.*

O God, Father of our Lord Jesus Christ, look down in Thy favor and compassion upon the whole body of Thy faithful servants, whom Thou hast called into the fellowship of Thy Son.

Grant unto them a spirit of knowledge and understanding in Thy truth; endow them plenteously with faith, hope, and charity, and with all heavenly gifts; and may they abound in good works, that they may adorn the doctrine of God our Saviour. *Amen.*

Being perfectly joined together in the same mind and in the same judgment, may they live together in unity, peace, and love, bearing each other's burdens, and so fulfilling the law of Christ. *Amen.*

Build up Thy holy temple in the earth, O God, and fill it with Thy glory. Adorn and beautify Thy Church with the graces of Thy Spirit; that every member of the same may be unto honor and praise at the appearing of our Lord Jesus Christ. And this we ask in His name who is exalted Head over all things, and is the Saviour of the Church, which is His body. *Amen.*

Relieve the sick and the destitute; comfort the sorrowful; draw nigh, in Thy mercy and grace, to the dying; and let all the miserable find consolation and redemption in Thee, O God. *Amen.*

Defend and prosper our native land. May it be governed with wisdom and justice. Grant success to all its righteous enterprises. Let the people be obedient to Thy holy laws, living godly, righteous, and sober lives, to the glory of Thy name. *Amen.*

Give grace to Thy servant the President, and to all Magistrates, Judges, and Rulers, to all classes and conditions of men; that we may all fulfil our appointed tasks as under the eye of the great Master, and may in due time enter into the joy of our Lord. *Amen.*

Almighty and most merciful Father, we Thy unworthy creatures unite in giving thanks and praise

unto Thy name for Thy great goodness and mercy to us and to all men. Thou loadest us with benefits: all that we have is Thine: we ourselves are Thine. We acknowledge Thee, O Lord, as the bountiful giver of all the good things of this present life, but especially of that blessed hope of an everlasting inheritance, which Thou hast given us in Christ Jesus our Lord. From this time henceforth may we consecrate ourselves to Thy service in all things; living as those who are not their own, being bought with a price.
Amen.

Lesson from New Testament. Hymn. Sermon.

PRAYER.

Almighty and everlasting God, who hast placed us in this life, full of trials and tears, in order that we through the same may learn to give careful heed to Thy Word, and be made meet for Thy kingdom, we pray Thee, let Thy good Spirit dispose our hearts to seek in Thy dear Son our only consolation under all sorrows, and enable us to forget our grief and pain in the enjoyment of His peace and love; through Jesus Christ our Lord. *Amen.*

Doxology. Benediction.

Third Sunday.

AFTERNOON SERVICE.

[The congregation being assembled, the Minister may recite the following sentences.]

HUMBLE yourselves in the sight of the Lord, and He shall lift you up.

Blessed are the undefiled in the way, who walk in the law of the Lord.

Blessed are they that keep His testimonies, and that seek Him with the whole heart.

I will hear what God the Lord will speak; for He will speak peace unto His people, and to His saints: but let them not turn again to foolishness.

Having these promises, Brethren, let us draw near to the throne of grace with true hearts, in full assurance of faith. Let us pray.

FIRST PRAYER.

Almighty and most merciful Father, we bless Thee that we are permitted to approach Thy throne of grace through Jesus Christ, the great High-Priest of our profession; assured that Thou hearest prayer, and wilt bestow upon us all things needful, whether for the body or the soul, for the life that now is, and that which is to come.

Blot out all our sins, we beseech Thee, O Lord: cleanse us from all our iniquities. Give us a heart to fear and love Thee. So teach us that we may know Thy will; so strengthen us that we may perform it constantly, and may grow in grace, in wisdom, and in all goodness; to the glory of Thy name; through Jesus Christ our Lord. *Amen.*

Lord of all power and might, who workest effectually in them that believe, and givest Thy Holy Spirit unto them that obey Thee, look in mercy upon our ignorance and our manifold infirmities; and so guide and strengthen us, that we may take up our cross and follow Christ our Master; committing ourselves in faith and patience to Thee, the righteous Judge; that so losing our life, we may keep it unto life eternal. *Amen.*

Fill us with godly fear, lest we fail of the grace of God, and make shipwreck of faith and a good conscience. Deliver us from unbelief, and hardness of heart, and a seared conscience: from selfishness and pride, from hypocrisy and love of the world, and from all fleshly lusts and debasing passions. Let our hands be clean from violence and wrong; let our hearts be pure from evil thoughts and corrupt desires; that we may be sincere and without rebuke, and, our heart not condemning us, we may have confidence towards Thee.

Deliver us not, O God, into the hand of our enemies; keep us from the snares of the wicked. By well-doing may we put to silence the ignorance of foolish men; as free, and not using our liberty as a cloak of maliciousness, but as the servants of God.

O Lord, enrich us with the graces of Thy Spirit; clothe our souls with the robes of righteousness, and beautify them with the garments of salvation, that we may be accepted guests at the marriage supper of the heavenly King. *Amen.*

O Lord, who knowest that we have no power to help or deliver us in those dangers which beset us in this our earthly pilgrimage, we beseech Thee that Thou wouldest be our defence and deliverer, and our high tower to save us. Let our faith and hope be in Thee; and do Thou make us perfect in every good word and work, to the glory of Thy grace; through Jesus Christ our Lord, in whose name and words we say,

Our Father which art in heaven, Hallowed be Thy name. Thy kingdom come. Thy will be done in earth, as it is in heaven. Give us this day our daily bread. And forgive us our debts, as we forgive our debtors. And lead us not into temptation, but deliver us from evil: for Thine is the kingdom, and the power, and the glory, forever. *Amen.*

Psalter for the day. Hymn.

PRAYER.

O Lord, omnipotent and eternal God, who didst proclaim Thy law from Mount Sinai in terrible majesty, we give Thee thanks that the thunder, and the earthquake, and the fire are now past, and we are permitted to hear the still small voice of Thy grace speaking to us in the gospel.

Deliver us, O Lord, from the spirit of bondage and fear, and shed Thy love abroad in our hearts by the Holy Ghost; that we may serve Thee in peace and joy, hoping for Thy glorious promises, through Jesus Christ our Saviour. *Amen.*

Grant, we beseech Thee, O gracious God, that through faith in Thy Son Jesus Christ, who, at His first coming, died in the flesh to take away the sin of the world, our souls may be redeemed from their pollution and guilt; that when He shall appear the second time in glory, our corruptible bodies may put on incorruption, and our mortal flesh be clothed with immortality; that as we have borne the image of the earthly, we may also bear the image of the heavenly, and be made partakers of that kingdom which flesh and blood shall not inherit. And this we ask in His name, who was dead, and liveth for evermore, Christ Jesus our Lord. *Amen.*

We praise and bless Thy holy name, Father of mercies, and God of all grace, that Thou hast had compassion upon us, miserable sinners:

That Thou didst send Thy Son to seek and save us:

That He took on Him the form of a servant, and the likeness of sinful flesh, and fulfilled Thy law, and was obedient to all Thy will even unto death:

That He made propitiation for our sins; and when He had overcome the sharpness of death, He opened the kingdom of heaven to all believers:

That He sitteth at Thy right hand in glory everlasting:

That He will come again in glory and majesty to judge the quick and the dead; and will reign till all enemies are put under His feet:

That He is our Advocate with Thee; the Captain of our salvation; the author and finisher of our faith:

That He is touched with the feeling of our infirmities; having been, in all points, tempted as we are.

That He ever liveth to make intercession; and saveth to the uttermost them that come unto Thee by Him:

That Thou hast sent unto us the gospel of Thy grace; and hast permitted us to unite with Thy Church militant in calling upon Thy name, and learning the way of eternal life.

O God, who dwellest from eternity in light that is inaccessible and full of glory, we thank Thee that, by the manifestation of Thy Son in the flesh, Thou hast revealed Thyself unto us, so dispelling our ignorance, and guiding our steps in the ways of righteousness and peace.

Incline our hearts, we beseech Thee, to hear His voice who speaketh to us from heaven; to obey and follow Him who is the light of the world; that, being translated out of the kingdom of darkness, and redeemed from all the power of sin and death, we may at length receive Thy promises, and be made partakers of glory, honor, and immortality; through our Lord and Redeemer, Jesus Christ. *Amen.*

Almighty God, the Creator and Preserver of all mankind, we pray Thee to send forth into all lands the light of Thy truth; and grant that all men may receive it in faith and love, that their spirits may be saved in the day of the Lord. *Amen.*

More especially we pray for the whole estate of Christ's Church upon earth; that all who make profession of His religion may be fully instructed in the doctrine which is according to godliness; and, being delivered from superstition and impiety, from heresies and schisms, from love of the world, from slavery to the flesh and the devil, may they be united in the bonds of peace and love, and, by all righteous and holy living, make their calling and election sure, to Thy glory and praise. *Amen.*

We commit ourselves and all that are dear to us, our kindred, friends, and benefactors, and those who have desired to be remembered in our prayers, to Thy mercy and grace, and to the keeping of Thy good providence, O Lord our God. *Amen.*

Grant unto them and us that which is needful for

the present life, and with it bestow Thy blessing. Enrich us with patience and resignation, with cheerfulness and fortitude; and teach us, in whatever state we are, therewith to be content.

Cleanse our souls with the presence of Thy good and Holy Spirit: adorn them with the ornaments of Thy grace: sanctify us wholly, in spirit, and soul, and body; and preserve us blameless to the coming and kingdom of our Lord. *Amen.*

New Testament Lesson. Hymn. Sermon.

PRAYER.

Let Thy gospel, O Lord, come to us not in word only but in power, and in the Holy Ghost; that we may be guided into all the truth, and also may be strengthened unto all obedience and enduring of Thy will with joyfulness; that we may abound in the work of faith, and the labor of love, and the patience of hope, and so may be made meet to be partakers of Thy heavenly inheritance; through Jesus Christ our Lord. *Amen.*

O God, who dost not slumber or sleep, guard us all, in soul and body, during the night. *Amen.*

May we rest under the shield of Thy providence in the peace of a good conscience and in the hope of a better life when the night and sleep of death are passed. *Amen.*

Raise us up again, if it please Thee, O Father of our spirits, that we may still serve Thee and see the goodness of the Lord in the land of the living. And so may we spend all the days of our life, that we may have hope in our death, and may rise again to the life immortal; through Him who died for our sins and rose again for our justification, Jesus Christ our Redeemer. *Amen.*

Lighten our darkness, we beseech Thee, O Lord; and by Thy great mercy defend us from all perils and dangers of this night; for the love of Thy Son, our Saviour, Jesus Christ. *Amen.*

Hymn. Doxology. Benediction.

Fourth Sunday

MORNING SERVICE.

[*The congregation being assembled, the Minister may recite one or more of the following sentences.*]

GOD is greatly to be feared in the assembly of the saints, and to be had in reverence of all them that are about Him.

O worship the Lord in the beauty of holiness: fear before Him, all the earth.

I will hear what God the Lord will speak; for He will speak peace unto His people and to His saints; but let them not turn again to folly.

Open to me the gates of righteousness: I will go into them; and I will praise the Lord. Let us pray.

FIRST PRAYER.

O God, almighty and everlasting, we would draw near unto Thee with reverence and godly fear, in the name of Thy Son, our Mediator and Advocate, Jesus Christ; beseeching Thee to fulfil to us that promise which He gave to His disciples. that wherever two or three are gathered together in His name, He will be in the midst of them. *Amen.*

Let our sacrifices of prayer and praise be acceptable in Thy sight, O Lord, through Him who is the great High-Priest of our profession, and who hath consecrated for us a new and living way into the Holiest; that coming boldly unto the throne of grace, we might obtain mercy, and find grace to help in time of need. *Amen.*

We have grievously offended Thee, O Lord our heavenly Father, by our manifold sins and iniquities, transgressing Thy righteous laws and resisting Thy Holy Spirit. We acknowledge our guilt and misery in Thy sight; entreating Thee to pardon all our offences, and to create in us clean and contrite hearts; that henceforth, being redeemed from all iniquity, we may serve Thee in holiness and righteousness, to the glory of Thy name; through our only Saviour Jesus Christ. *Amen.*

We rejoice in Thy promises, O God: we hope in Thy Word. Being justified freely by Thy grace, may we be made heirs, according to the hope of everlasting life. And having this hope in us, may we cleanse ourselves from all filthiness both of the flesh and of the spirit, and perfect holiness in Thy fear; that the peace of God, which passeth all understanding, may keep our hearts and minds; through Jesus Christ. *Amen.*

From the night early awaketh our soul unto Thee,

O God; for the light of Thy commandments is upon the earth.

Knowing it is high time to awake out of sleep, for the day of Thy judgment slumbereth not, let us cast off the works of darkness, and put on us the armor of light, and walk as those who have renounced the hidden things of dishonesty, and all the unfruitful works of darkness. *Amen.*

Lead us in Thy truth, O God: teach us to do Thy will: guide our steps in the ways of righteousness and peace: defend us from all snares and dangers, and deliver us from the powers of darkness; that we may walk before God in the light of the living. O Lord, enlighten our eyes, lest we sleep the sleep of death.
Amen.

These things we ask in His name who is the resurrection and the life; who also taught us, when we pray, thus to say,

Our Father which art in heaven, Hallowed be Thy name. Thy kingdom come. Thy will be done in earth, as it is in heaven. Give us this day our daily bread. And forgive us our debts, as we forgive our debtors. And lead us not into temptation, but deliver us from evil: for Thine is the kingdom, and the power, and the glory, forever. *Amen.*

Psalter for the day. Lesson from Old Testament. Hymn.

SECOND PRAYER.

O Lord, our heavenly Father, who hast revealed Thine eternal power and godhead in the creation of the world, and dost continually display Thy glory in upholding and governing the same, we thank Thee for that more perfect revelation of Thy character and will, which Thou hast given us in Thy Word.

Grant, we beseech Thee, O Lord, that we, upon whom Thou hast made the beams of Thy grace and truth to shine, may walk worthy of our high vocation, and adorn the doctrine of God our Saviour, living soberly, righteously, and godly in this present world; not being weary in well-doing, or fainting when we are chastened of Thee; that when Christ, who is our life, shall appear, we may be found worthy to stand before the Son of man, and be made partakers of glory, honor, and immortality. *Amen.*

O eternal God, who didst in the beginning create man in Thine own image, and who, when we were dead in sins, didst send forth Thy Son into the world that we might live through Him, we magnify Thy great name that, by faith of Thy Christ, we are born again to a lively hope, and are made heirs of Thy incorruptible inheritance.

Do Thou, who art the inexhaustible fountain of light and life, and who, as on this day, didst bring again from the dead the Lord Jesus, grant that we, who have been baptized into His death, may be quickened and raised up through the mighty power of Thy Spirit; that being made free from sin, we may serve Thee, the living God, continually in newness of life, presenting our bodies living sacrifices, holy and acceptable, which is our reasonable service; through the same Jesus Christ, who, in the power of the Eternal Spirit, offered Himself without spot unto Thee, and is our great High-Priest and Advocate in the heavenly temple. *Amen.*

O God, who sustaineth our life from day to day, opening Thy bountiful hand to supply all our wants, we acknowledge with gratitude Thy unmerited goodness.

May we use Thy bounties with humility, temperance, and charity; may we eat and drink, may we do all things and enjoy all, to Thy glory; that our bodies may be strengthened for Thy service upon earth, and we may be prepared for that heavenly life, when Thou wilt feed our souls with the bread of Thine eternal truth, and refresh them forever from the fountain of Thine inexhaustible love; through Christ our Lord.
Amen.

Grant, O Lord, that we, whom Thou hast made rational creatures, may, through Thy grace, be delivered from the carnal mind, which is death, and from all the deeds of the flesh, and may serve Thee, the living God, in righteousness and purity all the days of our life upon earth; that in due time we may reign with Christ in that kingdom which flesh and blood shall not inherit; through Him who is our only Lord and Saviour. *Amen.*

O Thou great Master and Lord, whose are all things in heaven and earth, and who givest to every one as it seemeth meet unto Thy godly wisdom, grant us grace, we pray Thee, that we may diligently and faithfully employ the talents, whatever they are, which Thou hast committed to us for a season; that when the Lord shall come and reckon with His servants, we may render our account with joy, and not with grief. *Amen.*

Vouchsafe unto those that are rich in this world that they be not high-minded, or trust in uncertain riches, but in the living God, who giveth us all things richly to enjoy; that they be rich in good works, laying up a good foundation against the time to come, that they may lay hold on eternal life:

And unto Thy servants that are poor in this world, that they be poor in spirit, but rich in faith, and heirs of that kingdom which Thou hast promised to them that love Thee. *Amen.*

By Thy grace working in us, may we daily perform better the part Thou hast assigned us in the world, growing and increasing continually in faith and patience, in love to God and charity to men, in contentment, in resignation and submission to Thy will, in meekness, gentleness, and all holy dispositions and Christian graces; that when our last day upon the earth shall come, we may be found perfect and complete in all the will of God. *Amen.*

In all the work of our hands may we work Thy work; and in all our labors for the meat that perisheth, may we labor for that meat which endureth to eternal life, and so use this world as not abusing it, for the fashion of this world passeth away. *Amen.*

O God our Saviour, who willest that all men be saved through the knowledge and obedience of the truth, and hast given us commandment to make prayers and intercessions for all men, through Thy Son, the one Mediator between God and men, who gave Himself a ransom for all, we entreat Thee to look down in Thy tender mercy upon all the kindreds of the nations; to deliver them from ignorance and superstition, idolatry and wickedness, from cruelty and oppression, from want and misery. *Amen.*

Cause the light of Thy truth to shine in all the dark places of the earth, and hasten Thy kingdom; that the glory of the Lord may be revealed, and all flesh may see it together. *Amen.*

We pray for all that are in authority, that they may govern the people committed to them in wisdom and justice, and in Thy fear; for all Judges and Magistrates, that we may lead a quiet and peaceable life in godliness and honesty, adorning the doctrine of God our Saviour. *Amen.*

Look down, O merciful Father, upon all Thy creatures who are in sorrow, pain, sickness, or any other adversity. Sanctify and strengthen the living for Thy service upon earth: sanctify and strengthen the dying; that being washed from the stains of sin, and eased of the load of guilt and fear, they may be made ready for the unspeakable joys of Thy presence in heaven. Let their cry enter into Thine ears, O God of Sabaoth: Lord, receive their prayer, and hear our prayers for them. Send into their hearts Thy Holy Spirit, the Comforter, that they may rejoice in tribulation, and be made perfect in that love which casteth out fear; through Christ our Lord, who suffered and was tempted, and is able to succor us when we are tempted; who died, and hath taken away the victory of death and the sting of the king of terrors, and is gone before to prepare mansions for us in heaven, that where He is there we may be also. *Amen.*

Lesson from New Testament. Hymn. Sermon.

PRAYER.

Almighty and Eternal God, who hast placed us in this life full of temptations and conflicts, and hast armed us against them with the sword of faith in Thy Son, so that we in the power of His strength may, like Him, overcome the world and its mighty ones; we pray Thee give us Thy good Spirit, that He may establish us firmly in such faith and grace, and that we may abide steadfast in the same unto our life's end; through Jesus Christ our Lord. *Amen.*

Hymn. Doxology. Benediction.

Fourth Sunday.

AFTERNOON SERVICE.

[*The congregation being assembled, the Minister may recite the following sentences.*]

OUR help is in the name of the Lord, who made heaven and earth.

Thus saith the high and lofty One that inhabiteth eternity, whose name is Holy; I dwell in the high and holy place, with him also that is of a contrite and humble spirit, to revive the spirit of the humble, and the heart of the contrite.

Blessed are the people that know the joyful sound: they shall walk, O Lord, in the light of Thy countenance. Let us pray.

FIRST PRAYER.

O God, who lovest the gates of Zion more than all the dwellings of Jacob, and hast commanded us not to forsake the assembling of ourselves together, be merciful to us, we beseech Thee, and make us joyful in Thy house of prayer.

Grant us Thy grace, without which we cannot worship Thee acceptably. Deliver us from unbelief, and hardness of heart, from hypocrisy and love of the world, from the dominion of the flesh, and from the powers of darkness; and endow us with faith, hope, and charity, that we may worship Thee in spirit and in truth, for Thou seekest such to worship Thee.
Amen.

O God, merciful Father, who despisest not the sacrifices of a broken and contrite heart, and hast no pleasure in the death of the wicked, but rather that he should turn unto Thee, and live; look upon us in Thy compassion, we humbly entreat Thee; for we have sinned against heaven and before Thee, and are not worthy to be called Thy children. *Amen.*

Grant unto us repentance and remission of our sins, through Thy Son Jesus Christ; who was delivered for our offences, and was raised again for our justification, and is now exalted at Thy right hand, a prince and a Saviour. *Amen.*

O God, who Thyself workest in us and hast commanded us to work out our own salvation with fear and trembling, we bless Thee for that day of grace which Thou dost afford us, in which we may learn the lessons of holy obedience, and may be exercised in the work of faith, the labor of love, the patience of hope, and in all the discipline of temperance, justice, and godliness.

May we be diligent in every good work, doing with

our might what our hand findeth to do. Give us grace to be faithful in that trust which the Lord hath committed to us; that when He shall come, we may receive that sentence, Well done, good and faithful servants, enter ye into the joy of your Lord. *Amen.*

Father of mercies and God of all comfort, who didst, in the fulness of time, send Thy Son to be the consolation of Israel, and hast promised another Comforter to abide with us forever, send forth, we pray Thee, Thy Holy Spirit into our hearts, to enlighten, sanctify, and guide us; to strengthen us in every good word and work; to uphold us in all temptations and trials; to comfort us in all our sorrows and afflictions; to fill us with joy and peace in believing, that we may abound in hope through the power of the Holy Ghost. *Amen.*

Psalter for the day. Lesson from the Scriptures. Hymn.

SECOND PRAYER.

O God Almighty, who quickenest the dead, and who didst raise up our Lord Jesus Christ, and give Him glory, bestow upon us Thy grace, that, as we have been baptized into His body, we may also be made partakers of His Spirit, and may walk in newness of life.

And as Christ, being raised from the dead, dieth no more, neither hath death any more dominion over Him, may we, being made free from sin, serve Thee, the living God, continually, having our fruit unto holiness, and the end everlasting life; through our Redeemer and Lord, Jesus Christ.   *Amen.*

Bestow upon us, we pray Thee, O Lord, Thy enlightening, purifying, and strengthening grace; that we may grow in wisdom, in holiness, and in all goodness, setting Thee before us in all things, and doing Thy work as wise and faithful servants.   *Amen.*

Let not any iniquity have dominion over us; neither suffer our hearts to be hardened through the deceitfulness of sin; but do Thou lead us in Thy truth and guide us, for Thou art the God of our salvation.   *Amen.*

And knowing that the night cometh in which no man can work, and that after death is the judgment, when each one of us shall give account of himself unto Thee, may we lay aside every weight, and run without fainting the course of faith and obedience which is set before us; that in the end we may be found worthy to stand before the Son of man, and may receive that crown of righteousness which the Lord hath promised to them that love Him.   *Amen.*

Have mercy, we entreat Thee, O Lord, upon all Thy creatures, and, of Thy great goodness, deliver them from those miseries and evils by which any of them are oppressed, especially from the shades of ignorance, error, and unbelief, and from the chains of sin. Them that are dead in trespasses do Thou awaken unto repentance and newness of life; and let all who make profession of Christ's religion adorn

His doctrine by a conversation becoming the gospel. And let Thy kingdom come; let Thy will be done, from the rising to the setting of the sun. **Amen.**

We entreat Thee, O Father, mercifully to receive the prayers of Thy servants everywhere that call upon Thee for help and deliverance. And for this end, grant unto them the Spirit of Thy Son; that, lifting up holy hands without wrath and doubting, they may be heard in that they fear; and having learned obedience by the things they suffer, may they in due time be made partakers of Thy salvation; through our merciful High-Priest, Jesus Christ, who Himself suffered and was tempted, and is able to succor us when we are tempted. **Amen.**

Grant, we beseech Thee, O Lord, that we may so receive Thy Word into our hearts, that it may be unto us a savor of life unto life. By it may we be made wise unto salvation, and be thoroughly furnished unto all good works. **Amen.**

O Lord God Almighty, who art the framer of our bodies, and the Father of our spirits, and hast sent Thy Son Jesus Christ to redeem us from sin and death, give us Thy grace, we entreat Thee; that, being purified from all filthiness both of the flesh and of the spirit, we may perfect holiness in Thy fear, yielding our members instruments of righteousness unto Thee, as those that are alive from the dead; that when this earthly tabernacle is dissolved, we may be received into everlasting habitations, and be clothed upon with our house from heaven, according to that working whereby Christ is able to subdue all things unto Himself. *Amen.*

Bless our country, and make it prosperous in all good things. Forgive us all our sins; and turn from us all those evils which we have deserved. Thou hast not dealt with us as we have sinned, nor rewarded us according to our transgressions. *Amen.*

Guide and counsel the President and all persons invested with public authority, that they may discharge their several duties as the ministers of God.
Amen.

We beseech Thee, O Father, look in compassion upon Thy universal Church; and as Thou hast knit together Thine elect in one communion and fellowship, grant us grace to follow Thy blessed saints in all virtuous and godly living; that we may finally be united with them in Thy kingdom of glory. *Amen.*

O God, whose counsels are of old, even from everlasting, and all whose ways are righteousness and truth, we adore Thy unfathomable wisdom, Thy boundless goodness, Thy judgments, which are unsearchable. Known unto Thee are all Thy works from the beginning; and Thou bringest good out of evil, and light out of darkness, and makest even the wrath of man to praise Thee.

We thank Thee that, in the fulness of time, Thy Son hath been manifested to destroy the works of the devil; that the darkness is past, and the true light now shineth. Let the beams of Thy grace, which bringeth salvation, illuminate all the nations of the world. Let Thy truth, O God, make all the peoples free. *Amen.*

Hasten, we pray Thee, the coming and kingdom of Christ; that the whole creation, which groaneth under the bondage of corruption, may be delivered, and we, with all Thy saints departed, may receive the adoption, even the redemption of our bodies; that the saying which is written may be fulfilled, Death is swallowed up of victory. Oh, the depth of the riches, both of the wisdom and knowledge of God! How unsearchable are His judgments, and His ways past finding out! For of Him, and through Him, and to Him are all things; to whom be glory forever.
Amen.

Hymn. Sermon.

PRAYER.

God of all grace, and fountain of all wisdom, we humbly beseech Thee to illuminate our minds and purify our hearts, that we may know Thy truth and approve the things that are excellent.

Let us no longer be children in understanding, or be carried about with diverse and strange doctrines, ever learning, yet never able to come to the knowledge of the truth. Grant that we may be perfect men in Christ Jesus, Thy Word dwelling in us richly in all wisdom and spiritual understanding.

O Lord our heavenly Father, be pleased to establish our hearts with grace, according to the faith of God's elect and the truth that is after godliness — even as He hath taught us, who is Thy Word made flesh, Jesus Christ, the same yesterday, to-day, and forever. *Amen.*

O Thou that dwellest in unapproachable light, keep us Thy servants during the darkness and silence of the night, from all evil, whether of the body or the soul; for we know not what enemies and dangers compass us about: and, when the night and darkness of this life are passed away, grant that we may awake to behold the light of Thine eternal glory in the kingdom of heaven, with all Thy saints; through Him that loved us, and hath redeemed us with His precious blood, Jesus Christ our Lord. *Amen.*

Lighten our darkness, we beseech Thee, O Lord; and by Thy great mercy defend us from all perils and dangers of this night; for the love of Thy only Son, our Saviour, Jesus Christ. *Amen.*

Hymn. Doxology. Benediction.

Fifth Sunday

MORNING SERVICE.

[*The congregation being assembled, the Minister may recite the following sentences.*]

LET all the earth fear the Lord: let all the inhabitants of the world stand in awe of Him.

For He spake and it was done; He commanded and it stood fast. The eye of the Lord is upon them that fear Him; upon them that hope in His mercy.

The Lord is nigh unto all them that call upon Him: to all that call upon Him in truth.

He will fulfil the desire of them that fear Him: He also will hear their cry, and will save them.

Brethren, let us with humble and contrite hearts draw nigh to the throne of the heavenly grace, confessing our sins, acknowledging the great goodness and mercy of our God, and asking in faith those things that are good for us; in the name of our great High-Priest and Advocate. Jesus Christ. Let us pray.

FIRST PRAYER.

We bow before the footstool of Thy divine Majesty, O God, adoring Thee, the Lord of heaven and earth; of whom, and through whom, and to whom are all things; to whom be ascribed all might, majesty, and dominion, world without end.

All things are full of Thee. The heavens declare Thy glory: the earth is full of Thy riches: so also is the great and wide sea. The day is Thine; the night also is Thine: Thou hast prepared the light and the sun: Thou hast set all the borders of the earth: Thou hast made summer and winter. Who would not fear Thee, O Lord, and glorify Thy name? for Thou only art holy. *Amen.*

O God, who art exalted above all blessings and praise, and needest not our service, for all things in heaven and earth are Thine, grant that we, and all our brethren throughout the world, may worship Thee this day in spirit and truth, and may find acceptance with Thee, through our Advocate and Mediator Jesus Christ. *Amen.*

And vouchsafe unto us, in the comfort of Thy worship here, a foretaste of heavenly joy; that while we drink together of the cup of Thy grace and consolation, we may be prepared to drink it new with Christ in His kingdom. *Amen.*

Almighty God, Father of our Lord Jesus Christ, we thank and praise Thee that Thou didst raise up

Thy Son from the dead, that the darkness of death might be dispelled, and life and immortality be brought to light; whereby we are born again to a new and lively hope.

Being risen with Christ, may we set our affection on things above, where He is exalted and reigneth at Thy right hand; from whence also we look for His second and glorious appearing. **Amen.**

Quicken us, O Lord, by Thy Spirit, to unfeigned repentance, to faith, hope, charity, and all holy dispositions and Christian virtues; that having in us the mind that was in Christ, we may worship Thee with our hearts, as well as with our lips, offering to Thy divine Majesty the sacrifices of righteousness, acceptable through Jesus Christ our Lord. **Amen.**

Our Father which art in heaven, Hallowed be Thy name. Thy kingdom come. Thy will be done in earth, as it is in heaven. Give us this day our daily bread. And forgive us our debts, as we forgive our debtors. And lead us not into temptation, but deliver us from evil: for Thine is the kingdom, and the power, and the glory, forever. *Amen.*

Psalter for the day. Lesson from Old Testament. Hymn.

SECOND PRAYER.

We humble ourselves in the dust before Thee, O Lord, confessing our daily offences against Thy divine Majesty. Our hearts and lives are polluted with innumerable sins. Thy fear hath not been at all times before our eyes; neither have we loved Thee with all our hearts, nor studied to serve and glorify Thee.

We have not fulfilled that royal law which requires us to love our neighbor as ourselves, or followed after charity, and the things whereby one may edify another. We have set our affection on things below, and have laid up treasure upon the earth, contemning that incorruptible inheritance which is reserved in heaven for the sons of God.

Hide Thy face from our sins, and blot out all our iniquities. If Thou shouldest mark iniquities, O Lord, who could stand? But there is forgiveness with Thee that Thou mayest be feared, and plenteous redemption. *Amen.*

Almighty God, who art more ready to hear than we are to pray, and art wont to give more than either we deserve or desire, pour down upon us the abundance of Thy mercy; forgiving us those things of which our conscience is afraid, and giving us those good things which we are not worthy to ask, but for Thy mercy's sake, through Christ our Lord. *Amen.*

O Almighty Father, God of all the world, in the light of whose presence there is perpetual day, we Thy servants bless and praise Thee, who holdest our souls in life, and makest the outgoings of the morning and evening to rejoice.

As we live by Thy power, so we desire to walk according to Thy laws, to be defended by Thy providence, to be sanctified by Thy grace. Let this day, and all the days of our life, be holy and peaceable. Send Thy Holy Spirit, the Spirit of peace, to be the guide of our way, the guard of our souls and bodies; that we may spend the remaining portion of our life in blessing, and peace, and holiness. *Amen.*

Deliver us from all the temptations of the world, the flesh, and the devil. Take not Thy grace from us; let us never want Thy help in our need, or Thy comforts in the day of our danger and calamity. Try us not beyond our strength, nor afflict us beyond our patience, nor smite us but with a Father's rod. Thou art our rock and our strong salvation. Deliver us, O God, from the miseries of this world, and save us from the wrath to come. Rescue us from the evils we have done, and preserve us from the evil we have deserved. *Amen.*

Receive Thy servants who approach the throne of Thy grace, in the name of Jesus Christ. Give unto each of us that which is best for us: cast out all evil from within us: work in us a fulness of holiness, of wisdom, and spiritual understanding; and make us fruitful in every good work; that, living before Thee with undefiled bodies and sanctified spirits, we may be presented without spot and blameless at the coming of our Lord Jesus Christ and all His saints. *Amen.*

O Lord, whose blessed Son hath ascended into the heavens, leave not us Thy family comfortless, but send Thy Holy Spirit into our hearts; that, being taught and quickened, purified and strengthened, by Thy heavenly grace, we may faithfully and joyfully serve Thee, both in doing and suffering Thy will; through Him who suffered for us, and hath left us an example that we might follow His steps. *Amen.*

O God, who hast commanded us to watch and pray that we enter not into temptation, endue us, we beseech Thee, with sobriety, vigilance, and godly fear. Leave us not to our own weak and deceitful hearts; neither let us be seduced by the power of evil example; but may we put on the whole armor of God, that we may stand in the evil day. Succor us, O heavenly Father, in our time of trial and temptation, through the Spirit, by which Thy Son our Lord was led into the wilderness to be tempted of the devil; that, our conflict ended, angels may be sent to minister unto us, as heirs of that salvation which Thou hast promised to as many as obey and follow Him.
Amen.

Here a Hymn may be sung, after which the Lesson from the New Testament is read. Then follows

THIRD PRAYER.

O God, Father of mercies, we Thy unworthy servants unite with one heart and voice in giving thanks and praise unto Thee for all the goodness and grace which Thou hast showed unto us and all men. Thou didst create us in Thine own image; Thou hast preserved us by Thy good providence; Thou hast delivered us from dangers and from death; Thou hast kept our feet from falling, and our eyes from tears; Thou hast bountifully supplied our wants, and loaded us with benefits: above all, we magnify Thy great name in that Thou didst send Thy Son into the world, that we might not perish by reason of our sins, but be made heirs according to the hope of everlasting life.

Let Thy love, O Lord, constrain us henceforth to live as those who are not their own, that we may glorify Thee with our bodies and spirits which are Thine. *Amen.*

O God, who art a Spirit, and with whom no sacrifices are accepted but such as are spiritual and holy, grant unto us Thy heavenly grace, that we may present our bodies a living sacrifice, holy and acceptable; offering unto Thy divine Majesty day by day the reasonable service of Faith, Hope, Love, Patience, Submission, Zeal, and all the works of piety, righteousness, and sobriety; that at length we may be exalted to serve Thee as kings and priests in the heavenly temple; through Thy Son, who, in the eternal Spirit, offered Himself without spot unto Thee, and is exalted and reigneth at Thy right hand, the High-Priest of our profession, Christ Jesus. *Amen.*

Sovereign Master and Lord of the world, we commend to Thy protection and favor the powers that be established to rule among the nations; especially Thy servant our President.

Grant Thy grace to all that bear rule over us.

Qualify and dispose them to govern in wisdom and righteousness; and may their administration be so blessed of Thee, that, under it, the whole body of the people may have peace and prosperity; and may they enjoy Thy bounties with thankful hearts. *Amen.*

O Lord, our gracious God, we implore Thy mercy for all who may be in peril by sea or land; for widows and orphans; for the poor; for prisoners; for the bereaved, the sick, and the dying, and for all the afflicted and sorrowful. May it please Thee, merciful Father, to look upon them in Thy compassion, to strengthen, comfort, and deliver them; or, if it be Thy will that they now finish their course upon earth, receive their spirits into Thy rest, and crown them with heavenly glory. *Amen.*

Thou art the Maker and Saviour of all men; and Thou art rich in mercy unto all that call upon Thee. Extend, O Lord, the light of Thy gospel to all the nations of the earth; reclaim them from their errors and sins; abolish all doctrines and worship that are contrary to Thy truth; and let all men acknowledge Thee, the only true God, and Jesus Christ whom Thou hast sent; that, the darkness being past, the true light may shine forever. *Amen.*

Finally, O Lord, we beseech Thee to pour out Thy blessing upon us, our persons, our families, our occupations, and all our concerns and interests. Give us whatever is needful for this present life, and also for that which is to come; and deliver us from vain regrets, needless anxieties, and unbelieving fears. We are in Thy hand; we commit ourselves to Thee; Thou wilt not leave us or forsake us. May we be diligent and prudent in our several callings; and may they yield fruits to the supply of our need, to the comfort of our brethren, and to Thy glory. Let us not place our good in riches, pleasures, honors, or any of the things of this perishing world, but in Thy favor, in the peace and joy of Thy Spirit, and in the hope of everlasting life, which Thou hast promised to them that love Thee.

Mercifully receive our prayers, and send us an answer in peace; through Thy well-beloved Son, our Lord and Saviour, Jesus Christ. *Amen.*

Lesson from New Testament. Hymn. Sermon.

PRAYER.

O Lord, let our prayers come before Thee in the name of Him who is the Angel of the everlasting covenant, who alone is worthy to receive all the glory of our redemption; and for whose sake we entreat Thee to bless us and keep us this night, and all the days and nights of our existence upon earth: and when the golden bowl shall be broken, and the spirit shall return to Thee, and the dust to the dust as it was, may it be to each of us the commencement of a life of glory, happiness, and joy, that shall never know an end. *Amen.*

Hymn. Doxology. Benediction.

Fifth Sunday.

AFTERNOON SERVICE.

[The congregation being assembled, the Minister may recite the following sentences.]

THE sacrifices of God are a broken spirit: a broken and a contrite heart, O God, Thou wilt not despise.

I will arise, and go to my father, and will say unto him, Father, I have sinned against heaven, and before thee, and am no more worthy to be called thy son.

Brethren, let us search and try our ways, and turn again to the Lord. Let us lift up our heart with our hands to God in the heavens. Let us pray.

FIRST PRAYER.

O God, Father of our Lord Jesus Christ, of whom the whole family in heaven and earth is named, give unto us who now draw near to Thy presence the aids of Thy heavenly grace, that we may worship Thee with contrite, faithful, and obedient hearts; and grant that we may be acceptable in Thy sight, and may receive our petitions; for we present our supplications before Thee in His name, who is the great High-Priest of our profession, our Mediator and Advocate, Jesus Christ. *Amen.*

Almighty and everlasting God, Creator of the world, Father of angels and men;

Have mercy upon us.

Thou blessed and only Potentate, who dwellest in thick darkness, though Thou Thyself art light without darkness; incomprehensible, inscrutable; who seest all things, Thyself unseen; who knowest all, though Thou canst not be known;

Have mercy upon us.

Lord God, most merciful and gracious, who daily loadest us with benefits, and art good even to the unthankful and the evil;

Have mercy upon us.

Thou didst breathe into us Thy Spirit: Thou didst create us in the image of God, making us only a little lower than the angels, and putting all things under our feet; but the crown is fallen from our head, for we have rebelled against Thee;

Have mercy upon us.

Thou knowest our frame; Thou rememberest that we are dust;

O Lord, have mercy upon us.

We have sinned, we have done very wickedly, departing from the living God; transgressing in thought, word, and deed Thy most righteous laws, and resisting Thy Holy Spirit: therefore we cry unto Thee:

Lord, have mercy upon us.

Before Thee, the Judge of the world, and the Searcher of hearts, whose eyes behold the evil and the good, and to whom all things are naked and open, we do confess our sins, and acknowledge our great iniquity:

O Lord, we entreat Thee, have mercy upon us.

Our heavenly Father, who didst send forth Thy Son, in the fulness of time, to bring near Thy salvation, grant unto us repentance and remission of sins, according to the riches of Thy grace; and bless us by turning every one of us away from our iniquities:

Have mercy upon us.

Through Christ, Thy well-beloved Son, whom Thou didst deliver up for us all, that He, by the grace of God, should taste death for every man:

Have mercy upon us, and put away all our offences.

By His sufferings, death, and burial, let our sins be crucified, that, being redeemed from the power of the flesh and of the carnal mind, we may no longer live in death, or be slaves to sin in the lusts thereof:

Lord, have mercy upon us, and for Thy name's sake take away all our sin.

God, who quickenest all things, Lord and Giver of life, who didst bring again from the dead our Lord

Jesus, that great Shepherd of the sheep, quicken us, Thy people and sheep of Thy pasture, with divine and heavenly life; inspiring us with faith, hope, charity, patience, and all the fruits of the Spirit, that we may glorify Thee upon the earth, may edify and strengthen our brethren, may work out our own salvation, may grow in grace, and be faithful unto death; that in due time we may be presented faultless before the presence of Thy glory with exceeding joy, and receive that crown of righteousness which Thou hast promised to them that love Thee:

Lord, have mercy upon us, and grant us Thy peace: have mercy upon us, and grant us Thy salvation.

In all time of our adversity; in our sickness, pain, and fear; in perplexity and distress; when we suffer wrongfully, and in all time of our trial and temptation:

Have mercy upon us.

In our health and wealth; in our ease, prosperity, and honor; and when all men speak well of us

Lord, have mercy upon us.

In the joys and sorrows, and in all the changes of this mortal life; at the hour of our death, and in the day of judgment:

Have mercy upon us.

O God, who dwellest not in temples made with hands, for Thou inhabitest eternity; heaven is Thy throne and the earth Thy footstool, and both earth and heaven are full of Thy glory, we bless Thee that

Thou dost reveal Thyself to the pure in heart, and dwellest with humble and contrite spirits.

Cleanse our hearts, O Thou invisible King, that we may behold with unveiled face Thy glory, and may ourselves be changed into the same image. Cast out all our pollutions and idols, that we may be temples of God, dwelling-places of the most High; and, being filled with grace and truth, may we have communion with the Father and the Son, and so be made partakers of the divine nature, and comprehend the mystery of Thy unfathomable love, that we may be filled with all the fulness of God. *Amen.*

We magnify and praise Thy great name, O Lord our heavenly Father, for all the goodness and mercy which Thou hast bestowed upon us, and upon our brethren of the human family. Thou didst create us in Thine own image; Thou hast opened Thy hand and supplied all our wants and made our cup to run over; Thou hast also, in Thy paternal love, chastened us, to make us partakers of Thy holiness. But chiefly we give Thee thanks that when, through our disobedience, we had fallen from Thee, Thou didst ransom us by the sufferings and death of Jesus Christ Thy Son; through whom also Thou hast given us the blessed hope of everlasting life.

We acknowledge with gratitude Thy ever-watchful providence, Thy abounding mercy, Thy overflowing goodness, Thy unwearied patience: but we are sinners.

O God, whom we do daily offend by our manifold iniquities, have mercy upon us, and blot out all our sins. Let it please Thee not to cut us down as cumberers of the ground; but spare us, and so quicken us by Thy grace, that we may live no longer unto ourselves, but unto Him who died for us and rose again, and whom Thou hast exalted at Thy right hand, that He may be Lord both of the dead and of the living. *Amen.*

As Thou hast called us into the marvellous light of Thy kingdom, may we not walk in darkness: redeem us from ignorance, error, and unbelief, from unholy desires, evil passions, and unrighteous actions, and from all the power of sin, both in our souls and bodies, that we may know the glorious liberty of the children of God, serving Thee in peace, in assured hope, and in perfect love, which casteth out fear. *Amen.*

O God, Redeemer of Israel, who wentest before Thy Church in the wilderness in the fiery and cloudy pillar, guiding them to the rest which Thou hadst promised, we thank Thee that Christ our Passover is sacrificed for us, whereby we are redeemed from the house of bondage, and the dominion of Him that had the power of death. By the washing of regeneration and renewing of the Holy Ghost, may we be cleansed from all the pollutions of our natural state; and daily may we eat of the hidden manna, even the word of Thy truth, and be made strong for our journey through the wilderness by this bread which cometh down from heaven; till at length we enter Thy promised rest, that eternal inheritance which Thou hast prepared for all that love Thee, whither the Forerunner is for us entered, Jesus Christ our Lord. *Amen.*

Psalter for the day. Lesson from the Scriptures. Hymn. Sermon. Then follows

PRAYER.

O Thou great Master and Lord, who callest us to serve Thee that we may be free, and art intrusting Thy talents to us for a season, grant us mercy to be faithful even in that which is least, not wasting or burying Thy talent, but improving it to Thy glory; that when the Lord shall reckon with us, we may be found good and faithful servants, and may enter into the joy of our Lord. *Amen.*

O Lord our heavenly Father, who hast taught us that there is one Body, even as there is one Spirit and one Lord, one Faith and one Baptism, one God and Father of us all, we lift up our hearts unto Thee on behalf of all that are called by Thy name. Let Thy blessing descend upon the whole Church; preserve her in truth and peace, in unity and safety, in all storms and against all temptations; that she, offering to Thy glory the never-ceasing sacrifice of prayer and thanksgiving and all holy obedience, may advance the honor of her Lord, and be filled with His Spirit, and partake of His glory. *Amen.*

Endow the ministers of Thy Word, and the pastors of Thy flock, with faith and wisdom, with charity and zeal, that Thy saints may be built up in their holy faith, and may abound in good works, to Thy glory and praise. *Amen.*

God of all grace and consolation, look down, we humbly entreat Thee, upon the sick, the sorrowful, and the dying; upon widows and orphans; upon the despairing and the tempted, and upon all who are in danger or perplexity, distress or tribulation. Hear their cry, O Lord; and for Thy mercy's sake deliver and save them; and us also, for we are men of like passions, and compassed about with infirmity and danger. May we not be high-minded, but fear, that we may stand in the evil day. *Amen.*

O Thou immortal King, with whom do live the spirits of them that depart hence in the Lord, and with whom the souls of the faithful, after they are delivered from the burden of the flesh, are in joy and felicity, we give Thee thanks for all those who lived in this world in obedience to Thy commands, and died in the hope of Thy promises, and now sleep in Jesus, waiting for His second and glorious appearing.

Let not us sorrow as others who have no hope. Thou art not the God of the dead but of the living; and Thy children, though dead unto us, still live unto Thee. We entreat Thee, O God, our Father and their Father, so to guide and sanctify us who are still in the body, that we also in due time may be gathered

unto the general assembly and church of the first-born, whose names are written in heaven, to live in everlasting joy, and reign with Christ and His saints, in the glory of Thy kingdom, world without end.
Amen.

O God, who art the Author of all being and all blessedness, the Fountain of our life and intelligence, and all our good; — for all comes from Thee, the creatures are but instruments of Thy grace, and messengers of Thy mercy; — we render unto Thee all praise and glory. Thou art the first and the last, the beginning and the end, the life and perfection of all things; who comprehendest and fillest all, yet canst not Thyself be comprehended; who art above all, through all, in all. Thou remainest unshaken, the eternal Rock, while the stream of creation rushes on in endless succession and ceaseless change, the invisible Spectator, the silent Witness of all good and evil; before the mountains were brought forth, or ever Thou hadst formed the earth and the world, from everlasting to everlasting Thou art God. *Amen.*

Our days and weeks glide swiftly away, reminding us of the end of our days, and the night which is at hand, when we shall cease from all our earthly cares and labors, and lie down in the dust in silence and darkness.

May we, by Thy grace, O Lord, so redeem the time of our visitation, that we shall close our eyes upon this world without sorrow or fear, and sleep in Jesus, our flesh resting in hope of Thy promises; that when the day of God shall dawn, we may arise with joy, and put on immortality, being redeemed from all the power of corruption, and made like unto the Son of God; that we, with all Thy saints, may live and reign with Him; who died for us and rose again, and liveth and reigneth with Thee the Father, in the unity of the Eternal Spirit, world without end. *Amen.*

O Thou that dwellest in unapproachable light, keep us Thy servants, and all that are dear to us, during the darkness and silence of the night, from all evil, whether of the body or the soul; for Thou only knowest our dangers, and Thou only canst defend and save us. And when the night and darkness of this life are passed away, grant that we may awake and behold the light of Thine eternal glory in the kingdom of heaven; through Him that loved us, and hath redeemed us from darkness, sin, and death, Jesus Christ our Lord. *Amen.*

Doxology. Benediction.

Sixth Sunday.

MORNING SERVICE.

The Minister shall begin the Morning Prayer, by reading one or more of the following sentences of Scripture.

THE Lord is in His holy temple; let all the earth keep silence before Him.

From the rising of the sun even unto the going down of the same, my Name shall be great among the Gentiles; and in every place incense shall be offered unto my Name, and a pure offering: for my Name shall be great among the heathen, saith the Lord of hosts.

Let the words of my mouth, and the meditation of my heart, be always acceptable in Thy sight, O Lord, my strength and my Redeemer.

When the wicked man turneth away from his wickedness that he hath committed, and doeth that which is lawful and right, he shall save his soul alive.

I acknowledge my transgressions; and my sin is ever before me.

Hide Thy face from my sins; and blot out all mine iniquities.

The sacrifices of God are a broken spirit: a broken and a contrite heart, O God, Thou wilt not despise.

Rend your heart, and not your garments, and turn unto the Lord your God; for He is gracious and merciful, slow to anger, and of great kindness, and repenteth Him of the evil.

To the Lord our God belong mercies and forgivenesses, though we have rebelled against Him; neither have we obeyed the voice of the Lord our God, to walk in His laws which He set before us.

O Lord, correct me, but with judgment; not in Thine anger, lest Thou bring me to nothing.

Repent ye; for the Kingdom of Heaven is at hand.

I will arise, and go to my father, and will say unto him, Father, I have sinned against heaven, and before thee, and am no more worthy to be called thy son.

Enter not into judgment with Thy servant, O Lord; for in Thy sight shall no man living be justified.

If we say that we have no sin, we deceive ourselves, and the truth is not in us; but if we confess our sins, God is faithful and just to forgive us our sins, and to cleanse us from all unrighteousness.

Then the Minister shall say,

Dearly beloved brethren, the Scripture moveth us, in sundry places, to acknowledge and confess our manifold sins and wickedness; and that we should not dissemble nor cloak them before the face of Almighty God our heavenly Father; but confess them with an humble, lowly, penitent, and obedient heart; to the end that we may obtain forgiveness of the same, by His infinite goodness and mercy. And although we ought, at all times, humbly to acknowledge our sins before God; yet ought we chiefly so to do, when we assemble and meet together to render thanks for the great benefits that we have received at His hands, to set forth His most worthy praise, to hear His most holy Word, and to ask those things which are requisite and necessary, as well for the body as the soul. Wherefore I pray and beseech you, as many as are present, to accompany me with a pure heart, and humble voice, unto the throne of the heavenly grace, saying,

A General Confession.

To be said by the whole Congregation, after the Minister, all kneeling.

Almighty and most merciful Father; we have erred, and strayed from Thy ways like lost sheep. We have followed too much the devices and desires of our own hearts. We have offended against Thy holy laws. We have left undone those things which we ought to have done; and we have done those things which we ought not to have done; and there is no health in us. But Thou, O Lord, have mercy upon us, miserable offenders. Spare Thou those; O

God, who confess their faults. Restore Thou those who are penitent; according to Thy promises declared unto mankind in Christ Jesus our Lord. And grant, O most merciful Father, for His sake; that we may hereafter live a godly, righteous, and sober life, to the glory of Thy holy Name. *Amen.*

Then the Minister shall kneel, and say the Lord's Prayer; the People still kneeling, and repeating it with him.

Our Father which art in heaven, Hallowed be Thy name. Thy kingdom come. Thy will be done in earth, as it is in heaven. Give us this day our daily bread. And forgive us our debts, as we forgive our debtors. And lead us not into temptation, but deliver us from evil: for Thine is the kingdom, and the power, and the glory, forever. *Amen.*

Then likewise he shall say,

O Lord, open Thou our lips.

Answer. And our mouths shall show forth Thy praise.

Here, all standing up, the Minister shall say,

Glory be to the Father, and to the Son, and to the Holy Ghost;

Answer. As it was in the beginning, is now, and ever shall be, world without end. *Amen.*

Minister. Praise ye the Lord.

Answer. The Lord's Name be praised.

Then may be said or sung the following Anthem.

Venite, exultemus Domino.

O come, let us sing unto the Lord; let us heartily rejoice in the strength of our salvation.

Let us come before His presence with thanksgiving; and show ourselves glad in Him with psalms.

For the Lord is a great God; and a great King above all gods.

In His hand are all the corners of the earth; and the strength of the hills is His also.

The sea is His, and He made it; and His hands prepared the dry land.

O come, let us worship and fall down, and kneel before the Lord our Maker.

For He is the Lord our God; and we are the people of His pasture, and the sheep of His hand.

O worship the Lord in the beauty of holiness; let the whole earth stand in awe of Him.

For He cometh, for He cometh to judge the earth; and with righteousness to judge the world, and the people with His truth.

Then shall follow the Psalter for the day, and then may be said or sung the Gloria Patri, *or else the* Gloria in excelsis.

Gloria in excelsis.

Glory be to God on high, and on earth peace, good will towards men. We praise Thee, we bless Thee, we worship Thee, we glorify Thee, we give thanks to

Thee for Thy great glory, O Lord God, heavenly King, God the Father Almighty.

O Lord, the only-begotten Son Jesus Christ; O Lord God, Lamb of God, Son of the Father, that takest away the sins of the world, have mercy upon us. Thou that takest away the sins of the world, have mercy upon us. Thou that takest away the sins of the world, receive our prayer. Thou that sittest at the right hand of God the Father, have mercy upon us.

For Thou only art holy; Thou only art the Lord; Thou only, O Christ, with the Holy Ghost, art most high in the glory of God the Father. *Amen.*

Then shall be read the first Lesson, after which shall be said or sung the following Hymn:

Te Deum laudamus.

We praise Thee, O God; we acknowledge Thee to be the Lord.

All the earth doth worship Thee, the Father everlasting.

To Thee, all Angels cry aloud; the Heavens, and all the Powers therein.

To Thee, Cherubim and Seraphim continually do cry,

Holy, Holy, Holy, Lord God of Sabaoth;

Heaven and earth are full of the Majesty of Thy Glory.

The glorious company of the Apostles praise Thee.

The goodly fellowship of the Prophets praise Thee.

The noble army of Martyrs praise Thee.

The holy Church throughout all the world doth acknowledge Thee;

The Father, of an infinite Majesty;

Thine adorable, true, and only Son;

Also the Holy Ghost, the Comforter.

Thou art the King of Glory, O Christ.

Thou art the everlasting Son of the Father.

When Thou tookest upon Thee to deliver man, Thou didst humble Thyself to be born of a Virgin.

When Thou hadst overcome the sharpness of death, Thou didst open the Kingdom of Heaven to all believers.

Thou sittest at the right hand of God, in the Glory of the Father.

We believe that Thou shalt come to be our Judge.

We therefore pray Thee, help Thy servants, whom Thou hast redeemed with Thy precious blood.

Make them to be numbered with Thy Saints, in glory everlasting.

O Lord, save Thy people, and bless Thine heritage.

Govern them, and lift them up forever.

Day by day we magnify Thee;

And we worship Thy Name ever, world without end.

Vouchsafe, O Lord, to keep us this day without sin.

O Lord, have mercy upon us, have mercy upon us.

O Lord, let Thy mercy be upon us, as our trust is in Thee.

O Lord, in Thee have I trusted; let me never be confounded.

Then shall be read, in like manner, the second Lesson, taken out of the New Testament.
And after that the following Psalm.

O be joyful in the Lord, all ye lands: serve the Lord with gladness, and come before His presence with a song.

Be ye sure that the Lord He is God; it is He that hath made us, and not we ourselves; we are His people, and the sheep of His pasture.

O go your way into His gates with thanksgiving, and into His courts with praise; be thankful unto Him, and speak good of His Name.

For the Lord is gracious, His mercy is everlasting; and His truth endureth from generation to generation.

Or this Hymn.

Blessed be the Lord God of Israel; for He hath visited and redeemed His people;

And hath raised up a mighty salvation for us, in the house of His servant David;

As He spake by the mouth of His holy Prophets, which have been since the world began;

That we should be saved from our enemies, and from the hand of all that hate us.

And after that, these Prayers following, all devoutly kneeling; the Minister first pronouncing,

The Lord be with you.

Answer. And with thy spirit.

Minister. Let us pray.

O Lord, show Thy mercy upon us.

Answer. And grant us Thy salvation.

Minister. O God, make clean our hearts within us.

Answer. And take not Thy Holy Spirit from us.

A Collect for Peace.

O God, who art the author of peace and lover of concord, in knowledge of whom standeth our eternal life, whose service is perfect freedom; Defend us Thy humble servants in all assaults of our enemies; that we, surely trusting in Thy defence, may not fear the power of any adversaries, through the might of Jesus Christ our Lord. *Amen.*

A Collect for Grace.

O Lord, our heavenly Father, Almighty and everlasting God, who hast safely brought us to the beginning of this day; Defend us in the same with Thy mighty power; and grant that this day we fall into no sin, neither run into any kind of danger; but that all our doings, being ordered by Thy governance, may be righteous in Thy sight; through Jesus Christ our Lord. *Amen.*

A Prayer for the President of the United States, *and all in Civil Authority.*

O Lord, our heavenly Father, the high and mighty Ruler of the universe, who dost from Thy throne behold all the dwellers upon earth; Most heartily we beseech Thee with Thy favor to behold and bless Thy servant The President of the United States, and all others in authority; and so replenish them with the grace of Thy Holy Spirit, that they may always incline to Thy will, and walk in Thy way. Endue them plenteously with heavenly gifts; grant them in health and prosperity long to live; and finally, after this life, to attain everlasting joy and felicity; through Jesus Christ our Lord.   *Amen.*

The following Prayers are to be omitted here, when the Litany is read.

A Prayer for the Clergy and People.

Almighty and everlasting God, from whom cometh every good and perfect gift; Send down upon our Bishops, and other Clergy, and upon the Congregations committed to their charge, the healthful Spirit of Thy grace; and, that they may truly please Thee, pour upon them the continual dew of Thy blessing. Grant this, O Lord, for the honor of our Advocate and Mediator, Jesus Christ.   *Amen.*

A Prayer for all Conditions of Men.

O God, the Creator and Preserver of all mankind, we humbly beseech Thee for all sorts and conditions of men; that Thou wouldest be pleased to make Thy ways known unto them, Thy saving health unto all nations. More especially we pray for Thy holy

Church universal; that it may be so guided and governed by Thy good Spirit, that all who profess and call themselves Christians may be led into the way of truth, and hold the faith in unity of spirit, in the bond of peace, and in righteousness of life. Finally, we commend to Thy fatherly goodness all those who are any ways afflicted or distressed, in mind, body, or estate; that it may please Thee to comfort and relieve them, according to their several necessities; giving them patience under their sufferings, and a happy issue out of all their afflictions. And this we beg for Jesus Christ's sake.   *Amen.*

THE LITANY.

O God the Father, of Heaven, have mercy upon us miserable sinners.

O God the Father, of Heaven, have mercy upon us miserable sinners.

O God the Son, Redeemer of the world, have mercy upon us miserable sinners.

O God the Son, Redeemer of the world, have mercy upon us miserable sinners.

O God the Holy Ghost, proceeding from the Father and the Son, have mercy upon us miserable sinners.

O God the Holy Ghost, proceeding from the Father and the Son, have mercy upon us miserable sinners.

O holy, blessed, and glorious Trinity, three Persons and one God, have mercy upon us miserable sinners.

O holy, blessed, and glorious Trinity, three Persons and one God, have mercy upon us miserable sinners.

Remember not, Lord, our offences; neither take Thou vengeance of our sins; spare us, good Lord, spare Thy people, whom Thou hast redeemed with Thy most precious blood, and be not angry with us for ever.

Spare us, good Lord.

From all evil and mischief; from sin; from the craft and assaults of the devil; from Thy wrath, and from everlasting damnation,

Good Lord, deliver us.

From all blindness of heart; from pride, vainglory, and hypocrisy; from envy, hatred, and malice, and all uncharitableness,

Good Lord, deliver us.

From all inordinate and sinful affections; and from all the deceits of the world, the flesh, and the devil,

Good Lord, deliver us.

From lightning and tempest; from plague, pestilence, and famine; from battle and murder, and from violent death,

Good Lord, deliver us.

From all sedition, privy conspiracy, and rebellion; from all false doctrine; from hardness of heart, and contempt of Thy Word and Commandment,

Good Lord, deliver us.

By the mystery of thy holy Incarnation, by Thy holy Nativity and Circumcision; by Thy Baptism, Fasting, and Temptation,

Good Lord, deliver us.

By Thine Agony and Bloody Sweat; by Thy Cross and Passion; by Thy precious Death and Burial; by Thy glorious Resurrection and Ascension; and by the coming of the Holy Ghost,

Good Lord, deliver us.

In all time of our tribulation; in all time of our prosperity; in the hour of death, and in the day of judgment,

Good Lord, deliver us.

We sinners do beseech Thee to hear us, O Lord God; and that it may please Thee to rule and govern Thy holy Church universal in the right way;

We beseech Thee to hear us, good Lord.

That it may please Thee to bless and preserve all Christian Rulers and Magistrates, giving them grace to execute justice, and to maintain truth;

We beseech Thee to hear us, good Lord.

That it may please Thee to illuminate all Pastors and Ministers of the Church with true knowledge and understanding of Thy Word; and that both by their preaching and their living they may set it forth, and show it accordingly;

We beseech Thee to hear us, good Lord.

That it may please Thee to send forth faithful laborers into thy harvest;

We beseech Thee to hear us, good Lord.

That it may please Thee to bless and keep all Thy people;

We beseech Thee to hear us, good Lord.

That it may please Thee to give to all nations unity, peace, and concord;

We beseech Thee to hear us, good Lord.

That it may please Thee to give us an heart to love and fear Thee, and diligently to live after Thy commandments;

We beseech Thee to hear us, good Lord.

That it may please Thee to give to all Thy people increase of grace to hear meekly Thy Word, and to receive it with pure affection, and to bring forth the fruits of the Spirit;

We beseech Thee to hear us, good Lord.

That it may please Thee to bring into the way of truth all such as have erred, and are deceived;

We beseech Thee to hear us, good Lord.

That it may please Thee to strengthen such as do stand; and to comfort and help the weak-hearted; and to raise up those who fall; and finally to beat down Satan under our feet;

We beseech Thee to hear us, good Lord.

That it may please Thee to succor, help, and comfort, all who are in danger, necessity, and tribulation;

We beseech Thee to hear us, good Lord.

That it may please Thee to preserve all who travel by land or by water, all sick persons, and young children; and to show Thy pity upon all prisoners and captives;

We beseech Thee to hear us, good Lord.

That it may please Thee to defend, and provide for,

the fatherless children, and widows, and all who are desolate and oppressed;

We beseech Thee to hear us, good Lord.

That it may please Thee to have mercy upon all men;

We beseech Thee to hear us, good Lord.

That it may please Thee to forgive our enemies, persecutors and slanderers, and to turn their hearts;

We beseech Thee to hear us, good Lord.

That it may please Thee to give and preserve to our use the kindly fruits of the earth, so that in due time we may enjoy them;

We beseech Thee to hear us, good Lord.

That it may please Thee to give us true repentance; to forgive us all our sins, and to endue us with the grace of Thy Holy Spirit to amend our lives according to Thy holy Word;

We beseech Thee to hear us, good Lord.

Son of God, we beseech Thee to hear us.

Son of God, we beseech Thee to hear us.

O Lamb of God, who takest away the sins of the world; have mercy upon us.

O Lamb of God, who takest away the sins of the world, grant us Thy peace.

> The Minister may, at his discretion, omit all that follows, to the Prayer, "We humbly beseech Thee, O Father," &c.

O Christ, hear us.

O Christ, hear us.

Lord, have mercy upon us.
Lord, have mercy upon us.
Christ, have mercy upon us.
Christ, have mercy upon us.
Lord, have mercy upon us.
Lord, have mercy upon us.

Then shall the Minister, and the People with him, say the Lord's Prayer.

Our Father who art in heaven, Hallowed be Thy name. Thy kingdom come. Thy will be done in earth, as it is in heaven. Give us this day our daily bread. And forgive us our trespasses, as we forgive those who trespass against us. And lead us not into temptation, but deliver us from evil. *Amen.*

Minister. O Lord, deal not with us according to our sins.

Answer. Neither reward us according to our iniquities.

Let us pray.

O God, merciful Father, who despiseth not the sighing of a contrite heart, nor the desire of such as are sorrowful; Mercifully assist our prayers which we make before Thee in all our troubles and adversities, whensoever they oppress us; and graciously hear us, that those evils which the craft and subtilty of the devil or man worketh against us, may, by Thy good providence, be brought to naught; that we Thy servants, being hurt by no persecutions, may evermore give thanks unto Thee in Thy holy Church; through Jesus Christ our Lord.

O Lord, arise, help us, and deliver us for Thy Name's sake.

O God, we have heard with our ears, and our fathers have declared unto us, the noble works that Thou didst in their days, and in the old time before them.

O Lord, arise, help us, and deliver us for Thine honor.

Glory be to the Father, and to the Son, and to the Holy Ghost;

Answer. As it was in the beginning, is now, and ever shall be, world without end. *Amen.*

From our enemies defend us, O Christ.
Graciously look upon our afflictions.
With pity behold the sorrows of our hearts.
Mercifully forgive the sins of Thy people.
Favorably with mercy hear our prayers.
O Son of David, have mercy upon us.
Both now and ever vouchsafe to hear us, O Christ.
Graciously hear us, O Christ; graciously hear us, O Lord Christ.

Minister. O Lord, let Thy mercy be showed upon us;

Answer. As we do put our trust in Thee.

Let us pray.

We humbly beseech Thee, O Father, mercifully to look upon our infirmities; and, for the glory of Thy Name, turn from us all those evils that we most justly have deserved; and grant, that in all our troubles we may put our whole trust and confidence in Thy mercy, and evermore serve Thee in holiness and pureness of living, to Thy honor and glory; through our only Mediator and Advocate, Jesus Christ our Lord. *Amen.*

A General Thanksgiving.

Almighty God, Father of all mercies, we, Thine unworthy servants, do give Thee most humble and hearty thanks for all Thy goodness and loving-kindness to us, and to all men. We bless Thee for our creation, preservation, and all the blessings of this life; but above all, for Thine inestimable love in the redemption of the world by our Lord Jesus Christ; for the means of grace, and for the hope of glory. And, we beseech Thee, give us that due sense of all Thy mercies, that our hearts may be unfeignedly thankful, and that we may show forth Thy praise, not only with our lips, but in our lives; by giving up ourselves to Thy service, and by walking before Thee in holiness and righteousness all our days; through Jesus Christ our Lord, to whom, with Thee and the Holy Ghost, be all honor and glory, world without end. *Amen.*

A Prayer of St. Chrysostom.

Almighty God, who hast given us grace at this time with one accord to make our common supplications unto Thee; and dost promise that when two or three are gathered together in Thy Name Thou wilt grant their requests; Fulfil now, O Lord, the desires and petitions of Thy servants, as may be most expedient for them; granting us in this world knowledge of Thy truth, and in the world to come life everlasting. *Amen.*

2 *Cor.* xiii. 14.

The grace of our Lord Jesus Christ, and the love of God, and the fellowship of the Holy Ghost, be with us all evermore. *Amen.*

Hymn. Sermon.
BENEDICTION.

The peace of God, which passeth all understanding, keep your hearts and minds in the knowledge and love of God, and of His Son Jesus Christ our Lord: And the Blessing of God Almighty, the Father, the Son, and the Holy Ghost, be amongst you, and remain with you always. *Amen.*

10*   H

Sixth Sunday.

AFTERNOON SERVICE.

The Minister shall begin the Evening Prayer, by reading one or more of the following sentences of Scripture.

THE Lord is in His holy temple; let all the earth keep silence before Him.

From the rising of the sun even unto the going down of the same, my Name shall be great among the Gentiles; and in every place incense shall be offered unto my Name, and a pure offering: for my Name shall be great among the heathen, saith the Lord of hosts.

Let the words of my mouth, and the meditation of my heart, be alway acceptable in Thy sight, O Lord, my strength and my Redeemer.

When the wicked man turneth away from his wickedness that he hath committed, and doeth that which is lawful and right, he shall save his soul alive.

I acknowledge my transgressions; and my sin is ever before me.

Hide Thy face from my sins; and blot out all mine iniquities.

The sacrifices of God are a broken spirit: a broken and a contrite heart, O God, Thou wilt not despise.

Rend your heart, and not your garments, and turn unto the Lord your God; for He is gracious and merciful, slow to anger, and of great kindness, and repenteth Him of the evil.

To the Lord our God belong mercies and forgivenesses, though we have rebelled against Him; neither have we obeyed the voice of the Lord our God, to walk in His laws which He set before us.

O Lord, correct me, but with judgment; not in Thine anger, lest Thou bring me to nothing.

Repent ye; for the Kingdom of Heaven is at hand.

I will arise, and go to my father, and will say unto him, Father, I have sinned against heaven, and before thee, and am no more worthy to be called thy son.

Enter not into judgment with Thy servant, O Lord; for in Thy sight shall no man living be justified.

If we say that we have no sin, we deceive ourselves, and the truth is not in us; but if we confess our sins, God is faithful and just to forgive us our sins, and to cleanse us from all unrighteousness.

Then the Minister shall say,

Dearly beloved brethren, the Scripture moveth us, in sundry places, to acknowledge and confess our manifold sins and wickedness; and that we should not dissemble nor cloak them before the face of Almighty God our heavenly Father; but confess them with an humble, lowly, penitent, and obedient heart; to the end that we may obtain forgiveness of the same, by His infinite goodness and mercy. And although we ought, at all times, humbly to acknowledge our sins before God; yet ought we chiefly so to do, when we assemble and meet together to render thanks for the great benefits that we have received at His hands, to set forth His most worthy praise, to hear His most holy Word, and to ask those things which are requisite and necessary, as well for the body as the soul. Wherefore I pray and beseech you, as many as are here present, to accompany me with a pure heart, and humble voice, unto the throne of the heavenly grace, saying —

A General Confession.

To be said by the whole Congregation, after the Minister, all kneeling.

Almighty and most merciful Father; we have erred, and strayed from Thy ways like lost sheep. We have followed too much the devices and desires of our own hearts. We have offended against Thy holy laws. We have left undone those things which we ought to have done; and we have done those things which we ought not to have done; and there is no health in us. But Thou, O Lord, have mercy upon us, miserable offenders. Spare Thou those, O God, who confess their faults. Restore Thou those who are penitent; according to Thy promises declared unto mankind in Christ Jesus our Lord. And grant, O most merciful Father, for His sake; that we may hereafter live a godly, righteous, and sober life, to the glory of Thy holy Name. *Amen.*

Then the Minister shall kneel, and say the Lord's Prayer; the People still kneeling, and repeating it with him, both here, and wheresoever else it is used in Divine Service.

Our Father which art in heaven, Hallowed be Thy name. Thy kingdom come. Thy will be done in earth, as it is in heaven. Give us this day our daily bread. And forgive us our debts, as we forgive our debtors. And lead us not into temptation, but deliver us from evil: For Thine is the kingdom, and the power, and the glory, forever. *Amen.*

Then likewise he shall say,

O Lord, open Thou our lips.

Answer. And our mouth shall show forth Thy praise.

Here, all standing up, the Minister shall say,

Glory be to the Father, and to the Son, and to the Holy Ghost;

Answer. As it was in the beginning, is now, and ever shall be, world without end. *Amen.*

Minister. Praise ye the Lord.

Answer. The Lord's Name be praised.

Then shall follow the Psalter for the day. Then the first Lesson; after which shall be said or sung the following Psalm.

Cantate Domino. Psalm xcviii.

O sing unto the Lord a new song; for He hath done marvellous things.

With His own right hand, and with His holy arm, hath He gotten Himself the victory.

The Lord declared His salvation; His righteousness hath He openly showed in the sight of the heathen.

He hath remembered His mercy and truth toward the house of Israel; and all the ends of the world have seen the salvation of our God.

Show yourselves joyful unto the Lord, all ye lands; sing, rejoice, and give thanks.

Praise the Lord upon the harp; sing to the harp with a psalm of thanksgiving.

With trumpets also and shawms, O show yourselves joyful before the Lord the King.

Let the sea make a noise, and all that therein is; the round world, and they that dwell therein.

Let the floods clap their hands, and let the hills be joyful together before the Lord; for He cometh to judge the earth.

With righteousness shall He judge the world, and the people with equity.

Or this.

Bonum est confiteri. Psalm xcii.

It is a good thing to give thanks unto the

Lord, and to sing praises unto Thy Name, O Most Highest;

To tell of Thy loving-kindness early in the morning, and of Thy truth in the night season;

Upon an instrument of ten strings, and upon the lute; upon a loud instrument, and upon the harp.

For Thou, Lord, hast made me glad through Thy works; and I will rejoice in giving praise for the operations of Thy hands.

Then a Lesson of the New Testament; and after that shall be sung or said this Psalm.

Deus misereatur. Psalm lxvii.

God be merciful unto us and bless us, and show us the light of His countenance, and be merciful unto us;

That Thy way may be known upon earth, Thy saving health among all nations.

Let the people praise Thee, O God; yea, let all the people praise Thee.

O let the nations rejoice and be glad; for Thou shalt judge the folk righteously, and govern the nations upon earth.

Let the people praise Thee, O God; yea, let all the people praise Thee.

Then shall the earth bring forth her increase; and God, even our own God, shall give us His blessing.

God shall bless us; and all the ends of the world shall fear Him.

Or this.

Benedic, anima mea. Psalm ciii.

Praise the Lord, O my soul; and all that is within me, praise His holy Name.

Praise the Lord, O my soul, and forget not all His benefits;

Who forgiveth all thy sin, and healeth all thine infirmities;

Who saveth thy life from destruction, and crowneth thee with mercy and loving-kindness.

O praise the Lord, ye Angels of His, ye that excel in strength; ye that fulfil His commandment, and hearken unto the voice of His Word.

O praise the Lord, all ye His hosts; ye servants of His that do His pleasure.

O speak good of the Lord, all ye works of His, in all places of His dominion; praise thou the Lord, O my soul.

And after that, these Prayers following, all devoutly kneeling; the Minister first pronouncing,

The Lord be with you.

Answer. And with thy spirit.

Minister. Let us pray.

O Lord, show Thy mercy upon us.

Answer. And grant us Thy salvation.

Minister. O God, make clean our hearts within us.

Answer. And take not Thy Holy Spirit from us.

SIXTH SUNDAY—AFTERNOON SERVICE.

Then the Prayers following.

A Collect for Peace.

O God, from whom all holy desires, all good counsels, and all just works do proceed; Give unto Thy servants that peace, which the world cannot give; that our hearts may be set to obey Thy commandments, and also that by Thee, we, being defended from the fear of our enemies, may pass our time in rest and quietness; through the merits of Jesus Christ our Saviour. *Amen.*

A Collect for Aid against Perils.

O Lord, our heavenly Father, by whose Almighty power we have been preserved this day; By Thy great mercy defend us from all perils and dangers of this night; for the love of Thy only Son, our Saviour, Jesus Christ. *Amen.*

A Prayer for the President of the United States, and all in Civil Authority.

O Lord, our heavenly Father, the high and mighty Ruler of the universe, who dost from Thy throne behold all the dwellers upon earth; Most heartily we beseech Thee with Thy favor to behold and bless Thy servant THE PRESIDENT OF THE UNITED STATES, and all others in authority; and so replenish them with the grace of Thy Holy Spirit, that they may always incline to Thy will, and walk in Thy way. Endue them plenteously with heavenly gifts; grant them in health and prosperity long to live; and finally, after this life, to attain everlasting joy and felicity; through Jesus Christ our Lord. *Amen.*

A Prayer for the Clergy and People.

Almighty and everlasting God, from whom cometh every good and perfect gift; Send down upon our Bishops, and other Clergy, and upon the Congregations committed to their charge, the healthful Spirit of Thy grace; and, that they may truly please Thee, pour upon them the continual dew of Thy blessing. Grant this, O Lord, for the honor of our Advocate and Mediator, Jesus Christ. *Amen.*

A Prayer for all Conditions of Men.

O God, the Creator and Preserver of all mankind, we humbly beseech Thee for all sorts and conditions of men; that Thou wouldest be pleased to make Thy ways known unto them, Thy saving health unto all nations. More especially we pray for Thy holy Church universal; that it may be so guided and governed by Thy good Spirit, that all who profess and call themselves Christians may be led into the way of truth, and hold the faith in unity of spirit, in the bond of peace, and in righteousness of life. Finally, we commend to Thy fatherly goodness all those who are any ways afflicted, or distressed, in mind, body, or estate; that it may please Thee to comfort and relieve them, according to their several necessities; giving them patience under their sufferings, and a happy issue out of all their afflictions. And this we beg for Jesus Christ's sake.   *Amen.*

A General Thanksgiving.

Almighty God, Father of all mercies, we, Thine unworthy servants, do give Thee most humble and hearty thanks for all Thy goodness and loving-kindness to us, and to all men. We bless Thee for our creation, preservation, and all the blessings of this life; but above all, for Thine inestimable love in the redemption of the world by our Lord Jesus Christ; for the means of grace, and for the hope of glory. And, we beseech Thee, give us that due sense of all Thy mercies, that our hearts may be unfeignedly thankful, and that we may show forth Thy praise, not only with our lips, but in our lives; by giving up ourselves to Thy service, and by walking before Thee in holiness and righteousness all our days; through Jesus Christ our Lord, to whom, with Thee and the Holy Ghost, be all honor and glory, world without end.   *Amen.*

A Prayer of St. Chrysostom.

Almighty God, who hast given us grace at this time with one accord to make our common supplications unto Thee; and dost promise that when two or three are gathered together in Thy Name Thou wilt grant their requests; Fulfil now, O Lord, the desires and petitions of Thy servants, as may be most expedient for them; granting us in this world knowledge of Thy truth, and in the world to come life everlasting. *Amen.*

2 Cor. xiii. 14.

The grace of our Lord Jesus Christ, and the love of God, and the fellowship of the Holy Ghost, be with us all evermore. *Amen.*

Hymn. Sermon.

Gloria in excelsis.

Glory be to God on high, and on earth peace, good will towards men. We praise Thee, we bless Thee, we worship Thee, we glorify Thee, we give thanks to Thee for Thy great glory, O Lord God, heavenly King, God the Father Almighty.

O Lord, the only-begotten Son Jesus Christ; O Lord God, Lamb of God, Son of the Father, that takest away the sins of the world, have mercy upon us. Thou that takest away the sins of the world, have mercy upon us. Thou that takest away the sins of the world, receive our prayer. Thou that sittest at the right hand of God the Father, have mercy upon us.

For Thou only art holy; Thou only art the Lord; Thou only, O Christ, with the Holy Ghost, art most high in the glory of God the Father. *Amen.*

BENEDICTION.

The peace of God, which passeth all understanding, keep your hearts and minds in the knowledge and love of God, and of His Son Jesus Christ our Lord: And the Blessing of God Almighty, the Father, the Son, and the Holy Ghost, be amongst you, and remain with you always. *Amen.*

To be Used at Pleasure.

THE APOSTLES' CREED.

I believe in God the Father Almighty, Maker of heaven and earth:

And in Jesus Christ His only Son our Lord; who was conceived by the Holy Ghost, born of the Virgin Mary; suffered under Pontius Pilate, was crucified, dead, and buried; He descended into hell, the third day He rose from the dead; He ascended into heaven, and sitteth on the right hand of God the Father Almighty; from thence He shall come to judge the quick and the dead.

I believe in the Holy Ghost; the holy Catholic Church, the Communion of Saints; the Forgiveness of sins; the Resurrection of the body; and the Life everlasting. *Amen.*

The Collect.

Almighty God, unto whom all hearts are open, all desires known, and from whom no secrets are hid; cleanse the thoughts of our hearts by the inspiration of Thy Holy Spirit, that we may perfectly love Thee, and worthily magnify Thy holy Name; through Christ our Lord. *Amen.*

THE TEN COMMANDMENTS.

Minister. God spake these words, and said; I am the Lord thy God: Thou shalt have none other gods but me.

People. Lord, have mercy upon us, and incline our hearts to keep this law.

Minister. Thou shalt not make to thyself any graven image, nor the likeness of any thing that is in heaven above, or in the earth beneath, or in the water under the earth. Thou shalt not bow down to them, nor worship them: for I the Lord thy God am a jealous God, and visit the sins of the fathers upon the children, unto the third and fourth generation of them that hate me; and show mercy unto thousands in them that love me, and keep my commandments.

People. Lord, have mercy upon us, and incline our hearts to keep this law.

Minister. Thou shalt not take the Name of the Lord thy God in vain: for the Lord will not hold him guiltless, that taketh His Name in vain.

People. Lord, have mercy upon us, and incline our hearts to keep this law.

Minister. Remember that thou keep holy the Sabbath-day. Six days shalt thou labor, and do all that thou hast to do; but the seventh day is the Sabbath of the Lord thy God. In it thou shalt do no manner of work; thou, and thy son, and thy daughter, thy man-servant, and thy maid-servant, thy cattle, and the stranger that is within thy gates. For in six days the Lord made heaven and earth, the sea, and all that in them is, and rested the seventh day: wherefore the Lord blessed the seventh day, and hallowed it.

People. Lord, have mercy upon us, and incline our hearts to keep this law.

Minister. Honor thy father and thy mother; that thy days may be long in the land which the Lord thy God giveth thee.

People. Lord, have mercy upon us, and incline our hearts to keep this law.

Minister. Thou shalt do no murder.

People. Lord, have mercy upon us, and incline our hearts to keep this law.

Minister. Thou shalt not commit adultery.

People. Lord, have mercy upon us, and incline our hearts to keep this law.

Minister. Thou shalt not steal.

People. Lord, have mercy upon us, and incline our hearts to keep this law.

Minister. Thou shalt not bear false witness against thy neighbor.

People. Lord, have mercy upon us, and incline our hearts to keep this law.

Minister. Thou shalt not covet thy neighbor's

house, thou shalt not covet thy neighbor's wife, nor his servant, nor his maid, nor his ox, nor his ass, nor any thing that is his.

People. Lord, have mercy upon us, and write all these Thy laws in our hearts, we beseech Thee.

The Minister may say,

Hear also what our Lord Jesus Christ saith:

Thou shalt love the Lord thy God with all thy heart, and with all thy soul, and with all thy mind. This is the first and great commandment. And the second is like unto it; Thou shalt love thy neighbor as thyself. On these two commandments hang all the Law and the Prophets.

Let us pray.

O Almighty Lord, and everlasting God, vouchsafe, we beseech Thee, to direct, sanctify, and govern, both our hearts and bodies, in the ways of Thy laws, and in the works of Thy commandments; that, through Thy most mighty protection, both here and ever, we may be preserved in body and soul; through our Lord and Saviour Jesus Christ. *Amen.*

PSALTER.

[

Selections from the Psalms.

FIRST DAY OF THE MONTH.

PSALM I.

BLESSED is the man that walketh not in the counsel of the ungodly, nor standeth in the way of sinners, nor sitteth in the seat of the scornful.

But his delight is in the law of the Lord; and in His law doth he meditate day and night.

And he shall be like a tree planted by the rivers of water, that bringeth forth his fruit in his season; his leaf also shall not wither; and whatsoever he doeth shall prosper.

The ungodly are not so: but are like the chaff which the wind driveth away.

Therefore the ungodly shall not stand in the judgment, nor sinners in the congregation of the righteous.

For the Lord knoweth the way of the righteous: but the way of the ungodly shall perish.

PSALM III.

Lord, how are they increased that trouble me! many are they that rise up against me.

Many there be which say of my soul, There is no help for him in God.

But Thou, O Lord, art a shield for me; my glory, and the lifter up of mine head.

I cried unto the Lord with my voice, and He heard me out of His holy hill.

I laid me down and slept; I awaked; for the Lord sustained me.

I will not be afraid of ten thousands of people, that have set themselves against me round about.

Arise, O Lord; save me, O my God: for Thou hast smitten all mine enemies upon the cheek-bone; Thou hast broken the teeth of the ungodly.

Salvation belongeth unto the Lord; Thy blessing is upon Thy people.

PSALM IV.

Hear me when I call, O God of my righteousness; Thou hast enlarged me when I was in distress; have mercy upon me, and hear my prayer.

O ye sons of men, how long will ye turn my glory into shame? how long will ye love vanity, and seek after leasing?

But know that the Lord hath set apart him that is godly for Himself: the Lord will hear when I call unto Him.

Stand in awe, and sin not: commune with your own heart upon your bed, and be still.

Offer the sacrifices of righteousness, and put your trust in the Lord.

There be many that say, Who will shew us any good? Lord, lift Thou up the light of Thy countenance upon us.

Thou hast put gladness in my heart, more than in the time that their corn and their wine increased.

I will both lay me down in peace, and sleep: for Thou, Lord, only makest me dwell in safety.

SECOND DAY OF THE MONTH.

PSALM VI.

O Lord, rebuke me not in Thine anger, neither chasten me in Thy hot displeasure.

Have mercy upon me, O Lord; for I am weak: O Lord, heal me; for my bones are vexed.

My soul is also sore vexed: but Thou, O Lord, how long?

Return, O Lord, deliver my soul: oh, save me for Thy mercies' sake.

For in death there is no remembrance of Thee: in the grave who shall give Thee thanks?

PSALM VIII.

O Lord our Lord, how excellent is Thy name in all the earth! who hast set Thy glory above the heavens.

Out of the mouth of babes and sucklings hast Thou ordained strength because of Thine enemies, that Thou mightest still the enemy and the avenger.

When I consider Thy heavens, the work of Thy fingers, the moon and the stars, which Thou hast ordained;

What is man, that Thou art mindful of him? and the son of man, that Thou visitest him?

For Thou hast made him a little lower than the angels, and hast crowned him with glory and honor.

Thou madest him to have dominion over the works of Thy hands; Thou hast put all things under his feet:

All sheep and oxen, yea, and the beasts of the field;

The fowl of the air, and the fish of the sea, and whatsoever passeth through the paths of the seas.

O Lord our Lord, how excellent is Thy name in all the earth!

PSALM XV.

Lord, who shall abide in Thy tabernacle? who shall dwell in Thy holy hill?

He that walketh uprightly, and worketh righteousness, and speaketh the truth in his heart.

He that backbiteth not with his tongue, nor doeth evil to his neighbor, nor taketh up a reproach against his neighbor.

In whose eyes a vile person is contemned; but he honoreth them that fear the Lord. He that sweareth to his own hurt, and changeth not.

He that putteth not out his money to usury, nor taketh reward against the innocent. He that doeth these things shall never be moved.

PSALM XVI.

Preserve me, O God: for in Thee do I put my trust.

The Lord is the portion of mine inheritance and of my cup: Thou maintainest my lot.

The lines are fallen unto me in pleasant places; yea, I have a goodly heritage.

I will bless the Lord, who hath given me counsel: my reins also instruct me in the night seasons.

I have set the Lord always before me: because He is at my right hand, I shall not be moved.

Therefore my heart is glad, and my glory rejoiceth: my flesh also shall rest in hope.

For Thou wilt not leave my soul in hell; neither wilt Thou suffer Thine Holy One to see corruption.

Thou wilt shew me the path of life: in Thy presence is fulness of joy; at Thy right hand there are pleasures for evermore.

THIRD DAY OF THE MONTH.

PSALM XXII.

My God, my God, why hast Thou forsaken me? why art Thou so far from helping me, and from the words of my roaring?

O my God, I cry in the daytime, but Thou hearest not; and in the night season, and am not silent.

But Thou art holy, O Thou that inhabitest the praises of Israel.

Our fathers trusted in Thee: they trusted, and Thou didst deliver them.

They cried unto Thee, and were delivered: they trusted in Thee, and were not confounded.

But I am a worm, and no man; a reproach of men, and despised of the people.

All they that see me laugh me to scorn: they shoot out the lip, they shake the head, saying,

He trusted on the Lord that He would deliver him: let Him deliver him, seeing He delighted in him.

Be not far from me; for trouble is near; for there is none to help.

Many bulls have compassed me: strong bulls of Bashan have beset me round.

They gaped upon me with their mouths, as a ravening and a roaring lion.

I am poured out like water, and all my bones are out of joint: my heart is like wax; it is melted in the midst of my bowels.

My strength is dried up like a potsherd; and my tongue cleaveth to my jaws; and Thou hast brought me into the dust of death.

But be not Thou far from me, O Lord: O my strength, haste Thee to help me.

Deliver my soul from the sword; my darling from the power of the dog.

Save me from the lion's mouth: for Thou hast heard me from the horns of the unicorns.

I will declare Thy name unto my brethren: in the midst of the congregation will I praise Thee.

Ye that fear the Lord, praise Him; all ye the seed of Jacob, glorify Him; and fear Him, all ye the seed of Israel.

For He hath not despised nor abhorred the affliction of the afflicted; neither hath He hid his face from him; but when he cried unto Him, He heard.

My praise shall be of Thee in the great congregation: I will pay my vows before them that fear Him.

The meek shall eat and be satisfied: they shall praise the Lord that seek Him: your heart shall live forever.

All the ends of the world shall remember and turn unto the Lord: and all the kindreds of the nations shall worship before Thee.

For the kingdom is the Lord's: and He is the Governor among the nations.

A seed shall serve Him; it shall be accounted to the Lord for a generation.

FOURTH DAY OF THE MONTH.

PSALM XXIV.

The earth is the Lord's, and the fulness thereof; the world, and they that dwell therein.

For He hath founded it upon the seas, and established it upon the floods.

Who shall ascend into the hill of the Lord? or who shall stand in His holy place?

He that hath clean hands, and a pure heart; who hath not lifted up his soul unto vanity, nor sworn deceitfully.

He shall receive the blessing from the Lord, and righteousness from the God of his salvation.

This is the generation of them that seek Him, that seek thy face, O Jacob.

Lift up your heads, O ye gates; and be ye lift up, ye everlasting doors; and the King of glory shall come in.

Who is this King of glory? The Lord strong and mighty, the Lord mighty in battle.

Lift up your heads, O ye gates; even lift them up, ye everlasting doors; and the King of glory shall come in.

Who is this King of glory? The Lord of hosts, He is the King of glory.

PSALM XXV.

Unto Thee, O Lord, do I lift up my soul.

O my God, I trust in Thee: let me not be ashamed, let not mine enemies triumph over me.

Yea, let none that wait on Thee be ashamed: let them be ashamed which transgress without cause.

Shew me Thy ways, O Lord; teach me Thy paths.

Lead me in Thy truth, and teach me: for Thou art the God of my salvation; on Thee do I wait all the day.

Remember, O Lord, Thy tender mercies and Thy loving-kindnesses: for they have been ever of old.

Remember not the sins of my youth, nor my transgressions: according to Thy mercy remember Thou me for Thy goodness' sake, O Lord.

Good and upright is the Lord: therefore will He teach sinners in the way.

The meek will He guide in judgment: and the meek will He teach His way.

All the paths of the Lord are mercy and truth unto such as keep His covenant and His testimonies.

For Thy name's sake, O Lord, pardon mine iniquity; for it is great.

What man is he that feareth the Lord? him shall He teach in the way that he shall choose.

His soul shall dwell at ease; and his seed shall inherit the earth.

The secret of the Lord is with them that fear Him; and He will shew them His covenant.

Mine eyes are ever toward the Lord; for He shall pluck my feet out of the net.

Turn Thee unto me, and have mercy upon me; for I am desolate and afflicted.

The troubles of my heart are enlarged: O bring Thou me out of my distresses.

Look upon mine affliction and my pain; and forgive all my sins.

Consider mine enemies; for they are many; and they hate me with cruel hatred.

O keep my soul, and deliver me: let me not be ashamed; for I put my trust in Thee.

Let integrity and uprightness preserve me; for I wait on Thee.

Redeem Israel, O God, out of all his troubles.

FIFTH DAY OF THE MONTH.

PSALM XXVII.

The Lord is my light and my salvation; whom shall I fear? the Lord is the strength of my life; of whom shall I be afraid?

Though an host should encamp against me, my heart shall not fear: though war should rise against me, in this will I be confident.

One thing have I desired of the Lord, that will I seek after; that I may dwell in the house of the Lord all the days of my life, to behold the beauty of the Lord, and to inquire in His temple.

For in the time of trouble He shall hide me in His pavilion: in the secret of His tabernacle shall He hide me; He shall set me up upon a rock.

And now shall mine head be lifted up above mine enemies round about me: therefore will I offer in His tabernacle sacrifices of joy; I will sing, yea, I will sing praises unto the Lord.

Hear, O Lord, when I cry with my voice: have mercy also upon me, and answer me.

When Thou saidst, Seek ye my face; my heart said unto Thee, Thy face, Lord, will I seek.

Hide not Thy face far from me; put not Thy servant away in anger: Thou hast been my help; leave me not, neither forsake me, O God of my salvation.

When my father and my mother forsake me, then the Lord will take me up.

Teach me Thy way, O Lord, and lead me in a plain path, because of mine enemies.

I had fainted, unless I had believed to see the goodness of the Lord in the land of the living.

Wait on the Lord: be of good courage, and He shall strengthen thine heart; wait, I say, on the Lord.

PSALM XXIX.

Give unto the Lord, O ye mighty, give unto the Lord glory and strength.

Give unto the Lord the glory due unto His name; worship the Lord in the beauty of holiness.

The voice of the Lord is upon the waters: the God of glory thundereth: the Lord is upon many waters.

The voice of the Lord is powerful; the voice of the Lord is full of majesty, and in His temple doth every one speak of His glory.

The Lord sitteth upon the flood; yea, the Lord sitteth King forever.

The Lord will give strength unto His people; the Lord will bless His people with peace.

PSALM XXXI.

In Thee, O Lord, do I put my trust; let me never be ashamed: deliver me in Thy righteousness.

Bow down Thine ear to me; deliver me speedily: be Thou my strong rock, for an house of defence to save me.

For Thou art my rock and my fortress; therefore for Thy name's sake lead me, and guide me.

Pull me out of the net that they have laid privily for me: for Thou art my strength.

Into Thine hand I commit my spirit: Thou hast redeemed me, O Lord God of truth.

I will be glad and rejoice in Thy mercy: for Thou hast considered my trouble; Thou hast known my soul in adversities;

And hast not shut me up into the hand of the enemy: Thou hast set my feet in a large room.

Have mercy upon me, O Lord, for I am in trouble: mine eye is consumed with grief: my strength faileth because of mine iniquity.

But I trusted in Thee, O Lord: I said, Thou art my God.

My times are in Thy hand: deliver me from the hand of mine enemies, and from them that persecute me.

Make Thy face to shine upon Thy servant: save me for Thy mercies' sake.

Oh how great is Thy goodness, which Thou hast

laid up for them that fear Thee; which Thou hast wrought for them that trust in Thee before the sons of men!

Thou shalt hide them in the secret of Thy presence from the pride of man: Thou shalt keep them secretly in a pavilion from the strife of tongues.

For I said in my haste, I am cut off from before Thine eyes: nevertheless Thou heardest the voice of my supplications when I cried unto Thee.

O love the Lord, all ye His saints: for the Lord preserveth the faithful, and plentifully rewardeth the proud doer.

Be of good courage, and He shall strengthen your heart, all ye that hope in the Lord.

SIXTH DAY OF THE MONTH.

PSALM XXXIII.

Rejoice in the Lord, O ye righteous: for praise is comely for the upright.

Praise the Lord with harp: sing unto Him with the psaltery and an instrument of ten strings.

Sing unto Him a new song; play skilfully with a loud noise.

For the word of the Lord is right; and all His works are done in truth.

He loveth righteousness and judgment: the earth is full of the goodness of the Lord.

By the word of the Lord were the heavens made; and all the host of them by the breath of His mouth.

He gathereth the waters of the sea together as an heap: He layeth up the depth in storehouses.

Let all the earth fear the Lord: let all the inhabitants of the world stand in awe of Him.

For He spake, and it was done; He commanded, and it stood fast.

The Lord bringeth the counsel of the heathen to nought: He maketh the devices of the people of none effect.

The counsel of the Lord standeth forever, the thoughts of His heart to all generations.

Blessed is the nation whose God is the Lord; and the people whom He hath chosen for His own inheritance.

The Lord looketh from heaven; He beholdeth all the sons of men.

From the place of His habitation He looketh upon all the inhabitants of the earth.

He considereth all their works.

Behold, the eye of the Lord is upon them that fear Him, upon them that hope in His mercy;

To deliver their soul from death, and to keep them alive in famine.

Our soul waiteth for the Lord: He is our help and our shield.

For our hearts shall rejoice in Him, because we have trusted in His holy name.

Let Thy mercy, O Lord, be upon us, according as we hope in Thee.

SEVENTH DAY OF THE MONTH.

PSALM XXXIV.

I will bless the Lord at all times: His praise shall continually be in my mouth.

My soul shall make her boast in the Lord: the humble shall hear thereof, and be glad.

O magnify the Lord with me, and let us exalt His name together.

I sought the Lord, and He heard me, and delivered me from all my fears.

They looked unto Him, and were lightened: and their faces were not ashamed.

This poor man cried, and the Lord heard him, and saved him out of all his troubles.

The angel of the Lord encampeth around about them that fear Him, and delivereth them.

O taste and see that the Lord is good: blessed is the man that trusteth in Him.

O fear the Lord, ye His saints: for there is no want to them that fear Him.

The young lions do lack, and suffer hunger: but they that seek the Lord shall not want any good thing.

Come, ye children, hearken unto me: I will teach you the fear of the Lord.

What man is he that desireth life, and loveth many days, that he may see good?

Keep thy tongue from evil, and thy lips from speaking guile.

Depart from evil, and do good; seek peace, and pursue it.

The eyes of the Lord are upon the righteous, and His ears are open unto their cry.

The face of the Lord is against them that do evil, to cut off the remembrance of them from the earth.

The righteous cry, and the Lord heareth, and delivereth them out of all their troubles.

The Lord is nigh unto them that are of a broken heart; and saveth such as be of a contrite spirit.

Many are the afflictions of the righteous: but the Lord delivereth him out of them all.

He keepeth all his bones: not one of them is broken.

Evil shall slay the wicked: and they that hate the righteous shall be desolate.

The Lord redeemeth the soul of His servants: and none of them that trust in Him shall be desolate.

EIGHTH DAY OF THE MONTH.

PSALM XXXVIII.

O Lord, rebuke me not in Thy wrath: neither chasten me in Thy hot displeasure.

For Thine arrows stick fast in me, and Thy hand presseth me sore.

For mine iniquities are gone over mine head: as an heavy burden they are too heavy for me.

I am troubled; I am bowed down greatly; I go mourning all the day long.

Lord, all my desire is before Thee; and my groaning is not hid from Thee.

My heart panteth, my strength faileth me: as for the light of mine eyes, it also is gone from me.

For in Thee, O Lord, do I hope: Thou wilt hear, O Lord my God.

For I will declare mine iniquity; I will be sorry for my sin.

PSALM XXXIX.

Lord, make me to know mine end, and the measure of my days, what it is; that I may know how frail I am.

Behold, Thou hast made my days as an handbreadth; and mine age is as nothing before Thee: verily every man at his best state is altogether vanity.

Surely every man walketh in a vain show: surely they are disquieted in vain: he heapeth up riches, and knoweth not who shall gather them.

And now, Lord, what wait I for? my hope is in Thee.

Deliver me from all my transgressions: make me not the reproach of the foolish.

I was dumb, I opened not my mouth; because Thou didst it.

Remove Thy stroke away from me: I am consumed by the blow of Thine hand.

When Thou with rebukes dost correct man for

iniquity, Thou makest his beauty to consume away like a moth: surely every man is vanity.

Hear my prayer, O Lord, and give ear unto my cry; hold not Thy peace at my tears: for I am a stranger with Thee, and a sojourner, as all my fathers were.

O spare me, that I may recover strength, before I go hence, and be no more.

NINTH DAY OF THE MONTH.

PSALM XL.

I waited patiently for the Lord; and He inclined unto me, and heard my cry.

He brought me up also out of an horrible pit, out of the miry clay, and set my feet upon a rock, and established my goings.

And He hath put a new song in my mouth, even praise unto our God: many shall see it, and fear, and shall trust in the Lord.

Blessed is that man that maketh the Lord his trust, and respecteth not the proud, nor such as turn aside to lies.

Many, O Lord my God, are Thy wonderful works which Thou hast done, and Thy thoughts which are to us-ward: they cannot be reckoned up in order unto Thee: if I would declare and speak of them, they are more than can be numbered.

Sacrifice and offering Thou didst not desire; mine

ears hast Thou opened: burnt-offering and sin-offering hast Thou not required.

Then said I, Lo, I come: in the volume of the book it is written of me,

I delight to do Thy will, O my God: yea, Thy law is within my heart.

Withhold not Thou Thy tender mercies from me, O Lord: let Thy loving-kindness and Thy truth continually preserve me.

For innumerable evils have compassed me about: mine iniquities have taken hold upon me, so that I am not able to look up; they are more than the hairs of mine head: therefore my heart faileth me.

Be pleased, O Lord, to deliver me: O Lord, make haste to help me.

Let all those that seek Thee rejoice and be glad in Thee: let such as love Thy salvation say continually, The Lord be magnified.

But I am poor and needy; yet the Lord thinketh upon me: Thou art my help and my deliverer; make no tarrying, O my God.

PSALM XLII.

As the hart panteth after the water brooks, so panteth my soul after Thee, O God.

My soul thirsteth for God, for the living God: when shall I come and appear before God?

My tears have been my meat day and night, while they continually say unto me, Where is thy God?

When I remember these things, I pour out my soul in me: for I had gone with the multitude, I went with them to the house of God, with the voice of joy and praise, with a multitude that kept holyday.

Why art thou cast down, O my soul? and why art thou disquieted in me? hope thou in God: for I shall yet praise Him for the help of His countenance.

Deep calleth unto deep at the noise of Thy waterspouts; all Thy waves and Thy billows are gone over me.

The Lord will command His loving-kindness in the daytime, and in the night His song shall be with me, and my prayer unto the God of my life.

I will say unto God my rock, Why hast Thou forgotten me?

O send out Thy light and Thy truth: let them lead me; let them bring me unto Thy holy hill, and to Thy tabernacles.

Then will I go unto the altar of God, unto God my exceeding joy: yea, upon the harp will I praise Thee, O God my God.

Why art thou cast down, O my soul? and why art thou disquieted within me? hope in God: for I shall yet praise Him, who is the health of my countenance, and my God.

TENTH DAY OF THE MONTH.

PSALM XLV.

My heart is inditing a good matter: I speak of the things which I have made touching the king: my tongue is the pen of a ready writer.

Thou art fairer than the children of men: grace is poured into Thy lips: therefore God hath blessed Thee forever.

Gird Thy sword upon Thy thigh, O most mighty, with Thy glory and Thy majesty.

And in Thy majesty ride prosperously because of truth and meekness and righteousness; and Thy right hand shall teach Thee terrible things.

Thine arrows are sharp in the heart of the king's enemies; whereby the people fall under Thee.

Thy throne, O God, is forever and ever: the sceptre of Thy kingdom is a right sceptre.

Thou lovest righteousness, and hatest wickedness: therefore God, Thy God, hath anointed Thee with the oil of gladness above Thy fellows.

I will make Thy name to be remembered in all generations: therefore shall the people praise Thee for ever and ever.

PSALM XLVI.

God is our refuge and strength, a very present help in trouble.

Therefore will not we fear, though the earth be removed, and though the mountains be carried into the midst of the sea.

Though the waters thereof roar and be troubled, though the mountains shake with the swelling thereof.

There is a river, the streams whereof shall make glad the city of God, the holy place of the tabernacles of the most High.

God is in the midst of her; she shall not be moved: God shall help her, and that right early.

The heathen raged, the kingdoms were moved: He uttered His voice, the earth melted.

The Lord of hosts is with us; the God of Jacob is our refuge.

Come, behold the works of the Lord, what desolations He hath made in the earth.

He maketh wars to cease unto the end of the earth; He breaketh the bow, and cutteth the spear in sunder; He burneth the chariot in the fire.

Be still, and know that I am God: I will be exalted among the heathen, I will be exalted in the earth.

The Lord of hosts is with us; the God of Jacob is our refuge.

PSALM XLVII.

O clap your hands, all ye people; shout unto God with the voice of triumph.

For the Lord most high is terrible; He is a great King over all the earth.

He shall choose our inheritance for us, the excellency of Jacob whom He loved.

God is gone up with a shout, the Lord with the sound of a trumpet.

Sing praises to God, sing praises : sing praises unto our King, sing praises.

For God is the King of all the earth : sing ye praises with understanding.

God reigneth over the heathen : God sitteth upon the throne of His holiness.

ELEVENTH DAY OF THE MONTH.

PSALM LV.

Give ear to my prayer, O God ; and hide not Thyself from my supplication.

Attend unto me, and hear me: I mourn in my complaint, and make a noise ;

Because of the voice of the enemy, because of the oppression of the wicked : for they cast iniquity upon me, and in wrath they hate me.

My heart is sore pained within me : and the terrors of death are fallen upon me.

Fearfulness and trembling are come upon me, and horror hath overwhelmed me.

And I said, Oh that I had wings like a dove! for then would I fly away, and be at rest.

Lo, then would I wander far off, and remain in the wilderness.

I would hasten my escape from the windy storm and tempest.

As for me, I will call upon God; and the Lord shall save me.

Evening, and morning, and at noon, will I pray, and cry aloud: and He shall hear my voice.

He hath delivered my soul in peace from the battle that was against me: for there were many with me.

God shall hear, and afflict them, even He that abideth of old. Because they have no changes, therefore they fear not God.

Cast thy burden upon the Lord, and He shall sustain thee: He shall never suffer the righteous to be moved.

PSALM LVII.

Be merciful unto me, O God, be merciful unto me: for my soul trusteth in Thee: yea, in the shadow of Thy wings will I make my refuge, until these calamities be overpast.

I will cry unto God most high; unto God that performeth all things for me.

He shall send from heaven, and save me from the reproach of him that would swallow me up. God shall send forth His mercy and His truth.

Be Thou exalted, O God, above the heavens; let Thy glory be above all the earth.

My heart is fixed, O God, my heart is fixed: I will sing and give praise.

Awake up, my glory; awake, psaltery and harp: I myself will awake early.

I will praise Thee, O Lord, among the people: I will sing unto Thee among the nations.

For Thy mercy is great unto the heavens, and Thy truth unto the clouds.

Be Thou exalted, O God, above the heavens: let Thy glory be above all the earth.

TWELFTH DAY OF THE MONTH.

PSALM LXII.

Truly my soul waiteth upon God: from Him cometh my salvation.

He only is my rock and my salvation; He is my defence; I shall not be greatly moved.

My soul, wait Thou only upon God; for my expectation is from Him.

He only is my rock and my salvation: He is my defence; I shall not be moved.

In God is my salvation and my glory: the rock of my strength, and my refuge, is in God.

Trust in Him at all times; ye people, pour out your heart before Him: God is a refuge for us.

Surely men of low degree are vanity, and men of high degree are a lie: to be laid in the balance, they are altogether lighter than vanity.

Trust not in oppression, and become not vain in robbery: if riches increase, set not your heart upon them.

God hath spoken once; twice have I heard this; that power belongeth unto God.

Also unto Thee, O Lord, belongeth mercy: for Thou renderest to every man according to his work.

PSALM LXVIII.

Let God arise, let His enemies be scattered: let them also that hate Him flee before Him.

As smoke is driven away, so drive them away: as wax melteth before the fire, so let the wicked perish at the presence of God.

But let the righteous be glad; let them rejoice before God: yea, let them exceedingly rejoice.

Sing unto God, sing praises to His name: extol Him that rideth upon the heavens by His name JAH, and rejoice before Him.

A Father of the fatherless, and a Judge of the widows, God is in His holy habitation.

God setteth the solitary in families: He bringeth out those which are bound with chains: but the rebellious dwell in a dry land.

O God, when Thou wentest forth before Thy people, when Thou didst march through the wilderness.

The earth shook, the heavens also dropped at the presence of God: even Sinai itself was moved at the presence of God, the God of Israel.

The chariots of God are twenty thousand, even thousands of angels: the Lord is among them, as in Sinai, in the holy place.

Thou hast ascended on high, Thou hast led captivity captive: Thou hast received gifts for men; yea, for the rebellious also, that the Lord God might dwell among them.

Blessed be the Lord, who daily loadeth us with benefits, even the God of our salvation.

Our God is the God of salvation; and unto God the Lord belong the issues from death.

THIRTEENTH DAY OF THE MONTH.

PSALM LXXI.

In Thee, O Lord, do I put my trust: let me never be put to confusion.

Deliver me in Thy righteousness, and cause me to escape: incline Thine ear unto me, and save me.

Be Thou my strong habitation, whereunto I may continually resort: Thou hast given commandment to save me: for Thou art my rock and my fortress.

Deliver me, O my God, out of the hand of the wicked, out of the hand of the unrighteous and cruel man.

For Thou art my hope, O Lord God: Thou art my trust from my youth.

By Thee have I been holden up from the womb: my praise shall be continually of Thee.

I am as a wonder unto many: but Thou art my strong refuge.

Let my mouth be filled with Thy praise and with Thy honor all the day.

Cast me not off in the time of old age; forsake me not when my strength faileth.

O God, be not far from me: O my God, make haste for my help.

But I will hope continually, and will yet praise Thee more and more.

My mouth shall show forth Thy righteousness and Thy salvation all the day.

I will go in the strength of the Lord God: I will make mention of Thy righteousness, even of Thine only.

O God, Thou hast taught me from my youth: and hitherto have I declared Thy wondrous works.

Now also when I am old and grayheaded, O God, forsake me not; until I have shewed Thy strength unto this generation, and Thy power to every one that is to come.

Thy righteousness also, O God, is very high, who hast done great things: O God, who is like unto Thee!

Thou, which hast shewed me great and sore troubles, shalt quicken me again, and shalt bring me up again from the depths of the earth.

Thou shalt increase my greatness, and comfort me on every side.

I will also praise Thee with the psaltery, even Thy truth, O my God: unto Thee will I sing with the harp, O Thou Holy One of Israel.

My lips shall greatly rejoice when I sing unto Thee; and my soul, which Thou hast redeemed.

My tongue also shall talk of Thy righteousness all the day long.

FOURTEENTH DAY OF THE MONTH.

PSALM LXXVII.

I cried unto God with my voice, even unto God with my voice; and He gave ear unto me.

In the day of my trouble I sought the Lord: my sore ran in the night, and ceased not: my soul refused to be comforted.

I remembered God, and was troubled: I complained, and my spirit was overwhelmed.

Thou holdest mine eyes waking: I am so troubled that I cannot speak.

I have considered the days of old, the years of ancient times.

I call to remembrance my song in the night: I commune with mine own heart: and my spirit made diligent search.

Will the Lord cast off forever? and will He be favorable no more?

Is His mercy clean gone forever? doth His promise fail for evermore?

Hath God forgotten to be gracious? hath He in anger shut up His tender mercies?

And I said, This is my infirmity: but I will remember the years of the right hand of the most High.

I will remember the works of the Lord: surely I will remember Thy wonders of old.

I will meditate also of all Thy work, and talk of Thy doings.

Thy way, O God, is in the sanctuary: who is so great a God as our God?

Thou art the God that doest wonders: Thou hast declared Thy strength among the people.

Thou hast with Thine arm redeemed Thy people, the sons of Jacob and Joseph.

The waters saw Thee, O God, the waters saw Thee; they were afraid: the depths also were troubled.

The clouds poured out water: the skies sent out a sound: Thine arrows also went abroad.

The voice of Thy thunder was in the heaven: the lightnings lightened the world: the earth trembled and shook.

Thy way is in the sea, and Thy path in the great waters, and Thy footsteps are not known.

Thou leddest Thy people like a flock by the hand of Moses and Aaron.

FIFTEENTH DAY OF THE MONTH.

PSALM LXXXV.

Lord, Thou hast been favorable unto Thy land: Thou hast brought back the captivity of Jacob.

Thou hast forgiven the iniquity of Thy people, Thou hast covered all their sin.

Thou hast taken away all Thy wrath: Thou hast turned Thyself from the fierceness of Thine anger.

Turn us, O God of our salvation, and cause Thine anger toward us to cease.

Wilt Thou not revive us again: that Thy people may rejoice in Thee?

Shew us Thy mercy, O Lord, and grant us Thy salvation.

I will hear what God the Lord will speak: for He will speak peace unto His people, and to His saints: but let them not turn again to folly.

Surely His salvation is nigh them that fear Him; that glory may dwell in our land.

Mercy and truth are met together; righteousness and peace have kissed each other.

Truth shall spring out of the earth; and righteousness shall look down from heaven.

Yea, the Lord shall give that which is good; and our land shall yield her increase.

Righteousness shall go before Him; and shall set in the way of His steps.

PSALM LXXXVI.

Bow down Thine ear, O Lord, hear me: for I am poor and needy.

Preserve my soul; for I am holy: O Thou my God, save Thy servant that trusteth in Thee.

Be merciful unto me, O Lord: for I cry unto Thee daily.

Rejoice the soul of Thy servant: for unto Thee, O Lord, do I lift up my soul.

For Thou, Lord, art good, and ready to forgive; and plenteous in mercy unto all them that call upon Thee.

Give ear, O Lord, unto my prayer; and attend to the voice of my supplications.

In the day of my trouble I will call upon Thee: for Thou wilt answer me.

Among the gods there is none like unto Thee, O Lord; neither are there any works like unto Thy works.

All nations whom Thou hast made shall come and worship before Thee, O Lord; and shall glorify Thy name.

For Thou art great, and doest wondrous things: Thou art God alone.

Teach me Thy way, O Lord; I will walk in Thy truth: unite my heart to fear Thy name.

I will praise Thee, O Lord my God, with all my heart: and I will glorify Thy name for evermore.

For great is Thy mercy toward me: and Thou hast delivered my soul from the lowest hell.

O God, the proud are risen against me, and the assemblies of violent men have sought after my soul; and have not set Thee before them.

But Thou, O Lord, art a God full of compassion, and gracious, long-suffering, and plenteous in mercy and truth.

O turn unto me, and have mercy upon me; give Thy strength unto Thy servant, and save the son of Thine handmaid.

Shew me a token for good; that they which hate me may see it, and be ashamed: because Thou, Lord, hast holpen me, and comforted me.

PSALM LXXXVII.

His foundation is in the holy mountains.

The Lord loveth the gates of Zion more than all the dwellings of Jacob.

Glorious things are spoken of thee, O city of God.

And of Zion it shall be said, This and that man was born in her: and the Highest Himself shall establish her.

The Lord shall count, when He writeth up the people, that this man was born there.

As well the singers as the players on instruments shall be there: all my springs are in thee.

SIXTEENTH DAY OF THE MONTH.

PSALM LXXXVIII.

O Lord God of my salvation, I have cried day and night before Thee:

Let my prayer come before Thee: incline Thine ear unto my cry;

For my soul is full of troubles: and my life draweth nigh unto the grave.

I am counted with them that go down into the pit: I am as a man that hath no strength:

Free among the dead, like the slain that lie in the grave, whom Thou rememberest no more: and they are cut off from Thy hand.

Thou hast laid me in the lowest pit, in darkness, in the deeps.

Thy wrath lieth hard upon me, and Thou hast afflicted me with all Thy waves.

Thou hast put away mine acquaintance far from me; Thou hast made me an abomination unto them: I am shut up, and I cannot come forth.

Mine eye mourneth by reason of affliction: Lord, I have called daily upon Thee, I have stretched out my hands unto Thee.

Wilt Thou shew wonders to the dead? shall the dead arise and praise Thee?

Shall Thy loving-kindness be declared in the grave? or Thy faithfulness in destruction?

Shall Thy wonders be known in the dark? and Thy righteousness in the land of forgetfulness?

But unto Thee have I cried, O Lord; and in the morning shall my prayer prevent Thee.

Lord, why casteth Thou off my soul? why hidest Thou Thy face from me?

I am afflicted and ready to die from my youth up: while I suffer Thy terrors I am distracted.

Thy fierce wrath goeth over me; Thy terrors have cut me off.

They came round about me daily like water; they compassed me about together.

Lover and friend hast Thou put far from me, and mine acquaintance into darkness.

SEVENTEENTH DAY OF THE MONTH.

PSALM LXXXIX.

I will sing of the mercies of the Lord forever: with my mouth will I make known Thy faithfulness to all generations.

For I have said, Mercy shall be built up forever: Thy faithfulness shalt Thou establish in the very heavens.

For who in the heaven can be compared unto the Lord? who among the sons of the mighty can be likened unto the Lord?

God is greatly to be feared in the assembly of the saints, and to be had in reverence of all them that are about Him.

O Lord God of hosts, who is a strong Lord like unto Thee? or to Thy faithfulness round about Thee?

Thou rulest the raging of the sea: when the waves thereof arise, Thou stillest them.

The heavens are Thine, the earth also is Thine: as for the world and the fulness thereof, Thou hast founded them.

The north and the south Thou hast created them: Tabor and Hermon shall rejoice in Thy name.

Thou hast a mighty arm: strong is Thy hand, and high is Thy right hand.

Justice and judgment are the habitation of Thy throne: mercy and truth shall go before Thy face.

Blessed is the people that know the joyful sound:

they shall walk, O Lord, in the light of Thy countenance.

In Thy name shall they rejoice all the day : and in Thy righteousness shall they be exalted.

EIGHTEENTH DAY OF THE MONTH.

PSALM XC.

Lord, Thou hast been our dwelling-place in all generations.

Before the mountains were brought forth, or ever Thou hadst formed the earth and the world, even from everlasting to everlasting, Thou art God.

Thou turnest man to destruction; and sayest, Return, ye children of men.

For a thousand years in Thy sight are but as yesterday when it is past, and as a watch in the night.

Thou carriest them away as with a flood; they are as a sleep: in the morning they are like grass which groweth up.

In the morning it flourisheth, and groweth up; in the evening it is cut down, and withereth.

For we are consumed by Thine anger, and by Thy wrath are we troubled.

Thou hast set our iniquities before Thee, our secret sins in the light of Thy countenance.

For all our days are passed away in Thy wrath: we spend our years as a tale that is told.

The days of our years are threescore years and ten;

and if by reason of strength they be fourscore years, yet is their strength labor and sorrow; for it is soon cut off, and we fly away.

Who knoweth the power of Thine anger? even according to Thy fear, so is Thy wrath.

So teach us to number our days, that we may apply our hearts unto wisdom.

Return, O Lord, how long? and let it repent Thee concerning Thy servants.

O satisfy us early with Thy mercy; that we may rejoice and be glad all our days.

Make us glad according to the days wherein Thou hast afflicted us, and the years wherein we have seen evil.

Let Thy work appear unto Thy servants, and Thy glory unto their children.

And let the beauty of the Lord our God be upon us: and establish Thou the work of our hands upon us; yea, the work of our hands establish Thou it.

NINETEENTH DAY OF THE MONTH.

PSALM XCIV.

The Lord knoweth the thoughts of man, that they are vanity.

Blessed is the man whom Thou chastenest, O Lord, and teachest him out of Thy law;

That Thou mayest give him rest from the days of adversity, until the pit be digged for the wicked.

For the Lord will not cast off His people, neither will He forsake His inheritance.

But judgment shall return unto righteousness: and all the upright in heart shall follow it.

Unless the Lord had been my help, my soul had almost dwelt in silence.

When I said, My foot slippeth; Thy mercy, O Lord, held me up.

In the multitude of my thoughts within me Thy comforts delight my soul.

The Lord is my defence; and my God is the rock of my refuge.

PSALM XCVI.

O sing unto the Lord a new song: sing unto the Lord, all the earth.

Sing unto the Lord, bless His name; shew forth His salvation from day to day.

Declare His glory among the heathen, His wonders among all people.

The Lord is great, and greatly to be praised: He is to be feared above all gods.

For all the gods of the nations are idols: but the Lord made the heavens.

Honor and majesty are before Him: strength and beauty are in His sanctuary.

Give unto the Lord, O ye kindreds of the people, give unto the Lord glory and strength.

Give unto the Lord the glory due unto His name: bring an offering, and come into His courts.

O worship the Lord in the beauty of holiness: fear before Him, all the earth.

Say among the heathen that the Lord reigneth: the world also shall be established that it shall not be moved: He shall judge the people righteously.

Let the heavens rejoice, and let the earth be glad; let the sea roar, and the fulness thereof.

Let the field be joyful, and all that is therein: then shall all the trees of the wood rejoice

Before the Lord: for He cometh, for He cometh to judge the earth: He shall judge the world with righteousness, and the people with His truth.

TWENTIETH DAY OF THE MONTH.

PSALM XCVII.

The Lord reigneth; let the earth rejoice; let the multitude of isles be glad thereof.

Clouds and darkness are round about Him: righteousness and judgment are the habitation of His throne.

A fire goeth before Him, and burneth up His enemies round about.

The heavens declare His righteousness, and all the people see His glory.

Confounded be all they that serve graven images, that boast themselves of idols: worship Him, all ye gods.

Zion heard, and was glad; and the daughters of Judah rejoiced because of Thy judgments, O Lord.

For Thou, Lord, art high above all the earth: Thou art exalted far above all gods.

Ye that love the Lord, hate evil: He preserveth the souls of His saints; He delivereth them out of the hand of the wicked.

Light is sown for the righteous, and gladness for the upright in heart.

Rejoice in the Lord, ye righteous; and give thanks at the remembrance of His holiness.

PSALM XCVIII.

O sing unto the Lord a new song; for He hath done marvellous things: His right hand, and His holy arm, hath gotten Him the victory.

The Lord hath made known His salvation: His righteousness hath He openly shewed in the sight of the heathen.

He hath remembered His mercy and His truth toward the house of Israel: all the ends of the earth have seen the salvation of our God.

Make a joyful noise unto the Lord, all the earth: make a loud noise, and rejoice, and sing praise.

Sing unto the Lord with the harp; with the harp, and the voice of a psalm.

With trumpets and sound of cornet make a joyful noise before the Lord, the King.

Let the sea roar, and the fulness thereof; the world, and they that dwell therein.

Let the floods clap their hands: let the hills be joyful together

Before the Lord; for He cometh to judge the earth: with righteousness shall He judge the world, and the people with equity.

PSALM C.

Make a joyful noise unto the Lord, all ye lands.

Serve the Lord with gladness: come before His presence with singing.

Know ye that the Lord He is God: it is He that hath made us, and not we ourselves; we are His people, and the sheep of His pasture.

Enter into His gates with thanksgiving, and into His courts with praise: be thankful unto Him, and bless His name.

For the Lord is good; His mercy is everlasting; and His truth endureth to all generations.

TWENTY-FIRST DAY OF THE MONTH.

PSALM CIII.

Bless the Lord, O my soul: and all that is within me, bless His holy name.

Bless the Lord, O my soul, and forget not all His benefits:

Who forgiveth all thine iniquities: who healeth all thy diseases;

Who redeemeth thy life from destruction; who crowneth thee with loving-kindness and tender mercies;

Who satisfieth thy mouth with good things; so that thy youth is renewed like the eagle's.

The Lord executeth righteousness and judgment for all that are oppressed.

He made known His ways unto Moses, His acts unto the children of Israel.

The Lord is merciful and gracious, slow to anger, and plenteous in mercy.

He will not always chide: neither will He keep His anger forever.

He hath not dealt with us after our sins; nor rewarded us according to our iniquities.

For as the heaven is high above the earth, so great is His mercy toward them that fear Him.

As far as the east is from the west, so far hath He removed our transgressions from us.

Like as a father pitieth his children, so the Lord pitieth them that fear Him.

For He knoweth our frame; He remembereth that we are dust.

As for man, his days are as grass: as a flower of the field, so he flourisheth.

For the wind passeth over it, and it is gone; and the place thereof shall know it no more.

But the mercy of the Lord is from everlasting to everlasting upon them that fear Him, and His righteousness unto children's children;

To such as keep His covenant, and to those that remember His commandments to do them.

The Lord hath prepared His throne in the heavens; and His kingdom ruleth over all.

Bless the Lord, ye His angels, that excel in strength, that do His commandments, hearkening unto the voice of His word.

Bless ye the Lord, all ye His hosts; ye ministers of His, that do His pleasure.

Bless the Lord, all His works in all places of His dominion: bless the Lord, O my soul.

TWENTY-SECOND DAY OF THE MONTH.

PSALM CIV.

Bless the Lord, O my soul. O Lord my God, Thou art very great; Thou art clothed with honor and majesty.

Who coverest Thyself with light as with a garment: Who stretchest out the heavens like a curtain:

Who layeth the beams of His chambers in the waters: Who maketh the clouds His chariot: Who walketh upon the wings of the wind:

Who maketh His angels spirits; His ministers a flaming fire:

Who laid the foundations of the earth, that it should not be removed forever.

O Lord, how manifold are Thy works! in wisdom hast Thou made them all: the earth is full of Thy riches.

So is this great and wide sea, wherein are things creeping innumerable, both small and great beasts.

There go the ships: there is that leviathan, whom Thou hast made to play therein.

These wait all upon Thee: that Thou mayest give them their meat in due season.

That Thou givest them they gather: Thou openest Thine hand, they are filled with good.

Thou hidest Thy face, they are troubled: Thou takest away their breath, they die, and return to their dust.

Thou sendest forth Thy spirit, they are created: and Thou renewest the face of the earth.

The glory of the Lord shall endure forever: the Lord shall rejoice in His works.

He looketh on the earth, and it trembleth: He toucheth the hills, and they smoke.

I will sing unto the Lord as long as I live: I will sing praise to my God while I have my being.

My meditation of Him shall be sweet: I will be glad in the Lord.

Bless thou the Lord, O my soul. Praise ye the Lord.

PSALM CV.

O give thanks unto the Lord; call upon His name: make known His deeds among the people.

Sing unto Him, sing psalms unto Him: talk ye of all His wondrous works.

Glory ye in His holy name: let the heart of them rejoice that seek the Lord.

Seek the Lord, and His strength: seek His face evermore.

Remember His marvellous works that He hath done; His wonders, and the judgments of His mouth;

O ye seed of Abraham His servant, ye children of Jacob His chosen.

He is the Lord our God: His judgments are in all the earth.

PSALM CVI.

Praise ye the Lord. O give thanks unto the Lord; for He is good: for His mercy endureth forever.

Who can utter the mighty acts of the Lord? who can shew forth all His praise?

Blessed are they that keep judgment, and he that doeth righteousness at all times.

Remember me, O Lord, with the favor that Thou bearest unto Thy people: O visit me with Thy salvation;

That I may see the good of Thy chosen, that I may rejoice in the gladness of Thy nation, that I may glory with Thine inheritance.

We have sinned with our fathers, we have committed iniquity, we have done wickedly.

Save us, O Lord our God, and gather us from among the heathen, to give thanks unto Thy holy name, and to triumph in Thy praise.

Blessed be the Lord God of Israel from everlasting to everlasting: and let all the people say, Amen. Praise ye the Lord.

TWENTY-THIRD DAY OF THE MONTH.

PSALM CVII.

O give thanks unto the Lord, for He is good: for His mercy endureth forever.

Let the redeemed of the Lord say so, whom He hath redeemed from the hand of the enemy;

And gathered them out of the lands, from the east, and from the west, from the north, and from the south.

They wandered in the wilderness in a solitary way; they found no city to dwell in.

Hungry and thirsty, their soul fainted in them.

Then they cried unto the Lord in their trouble, and He delivered them out of their distresses.

And He led them forth by the right way, that they might go to a city of habitation.

O that men would praise the Lord for His goodness, and for His wonderful works to the children of men!

For He satisfieth the longing soul, and filleth the hungry soul with goodness.

Such as sit in darkness and in the shadow of death, being bound in affliction and iron;

Because they rebelled against the words of God, and contemned the counsel of the Most High:

Therefore He brought down their heart with labor; they fell down, and there was none to help.

Then they cried unto the Lord in their trouble, and He saved them out of their distresses.

He brought them out of darkness and the shadow of death, and brake their bands in sunder.

Oh that men would praise the Lord for His goodness, and for His wonderful works to the children of men!

For He hath broken the gates of brass, and cut the bars of iron in sunder.

Fools, because of their transgression, and because of their iniquities, are afflicted.

Their soul abhorreth all manner of meat; and they draw near unto the gates of death.

Then they cry unto the Lord in their trouble, and He saveth them out of their distresses.

He sent His word, and healed them, and delivered them from their destructions.

Oh that men would praise the Lord for His goodness, and for His wonderful works to the children of men!

And let them sacrifice the sacrifices of thanksgiving, and declare His works with rejoicing.

They that go down to the sea in ships, that do business in great waters;

These see the works of the Lord, and His wonders in the deep.

For He commandeth, and raiseth the stormy wind, which lifteth up the waves thereof.

They mount up to the heaven, they go down again to the depths: their soul is melted because of trouble.

They reel to and fro, and stagger like a drunken man, and are at their wits' end.

Then they cry unto the Lord in their trouble, and He bringeth them out of their distresses.

He maketh the storm a calm, so that the waves thereof are still.

Then are they glad because they be quiet; so He bringeth them unto their desired haven.

Oh that men would praise the Lord for His goodness, and for His wonderful works to the children of men!

Let them exalt Him also in the congregation of the people, and praise Him in the assembly of the elders.

He turneth rivers into a wilderness, and the watersprings into dry ground;

A fruitful land into barrenness, for the wickedness of them that dwell therein.

He turneth the wilderness into a standing water, and dry ground into watersprings.

And there He maketh the hungry to dwell, that they may prepare a city for habitation;

And sow the fields, and plant vineyards, which may yield fruits of increase.

He blesseth them also, so that they are multiplied greatly; and suffereth not their cattle to decrease.

Again they are minished and brought low through oppression, affliction, and sorrow.

He poureth contempt upon princes, and causeth them to wander in the wilderness, where there is no way.

Yet setteth He the poor on high from affliction, and maketh Him families like a flock.

The righteous shall see it, and rejoice; and all iniquity shall stop her mouth.

Whoso is wise, and will observe these things, even they shall understand the loving-kindness of the Lord.

TWENTY-FOURTH DAY OF THE MONTH.

PSALM CXI.

Praise ye the Lord. I will praise the Lord with my whole heart, in the assembly of the upright, and in the congregation.

The works of the Lord are great, sought out of all them that have pleasure therein.

His work is honorable and glorious: and His righteousness endureth forever.

He hath made His wonderful works to be remembered: the Lord is gracious and full of compassion.

He hath given meat unto them that fear Him: He will ever be mindful of His covenant.

He hath shewed His people the power of His works, that He may give them the heritage of the heathen.

The works of His hands are verity and judgment; all His commandments are sure.

They stand fast forever and ever, and are done in truth and uprightness.

He sent redemption unto His people: He hath commanded His covenant forever: holy and reverend is His name.

The fear of the Lord is the beginning of wisdom: a good understanding have all they that do His commandments: His praise endureth forever.

PSALM CXII.

Praise ye the Lord. Blessed is the man that feareth the Lord, that delighteth greatly in His commandments.

Unto the upright there ariseth light in the darkness: he is gracious, and full of compassion, and righteous.

A good man sheweth favor, and lendeth: he will guide his affairs with discretion.

He hath dispersed, he hath given to the poor; his righteousness endureth forever; his horn shall be exalted with honor.

PSALM CXIII.

Praise ye the Lord. Praise, O ye servants of the Lord, praise the name of the Lord.

Blessed be the name of the Lord from this time forth and for evermore.

From the rising of the sun unto the going down of the same the Lord's name is to be praised.

The Lord is high above all nations, and His glory above the heavens.

Who is like unto the Lord our God, who dwelleth on high,

Who humbleth Himself to behold the things that are in heaven, and in the earth!

PSALM CXV.

Not unto us, O Lord, not unto us, but unto Thy name give glory, for Thy mercy, and for Thy truth's sake.

Wherefore should the heathen say, Where is now their God?

But our God is in the heavens: He hath done whatsoever He hath pleased.

Their idols are silver and gold, the work of men's hands.

Ye that fear the Lord, trust in the Lord: He is their help and their shield.

He will bless them that fear the Lord, both small and great.

The Lord shall increase you more and more, you and your children.

Ye are blessed of the Lord which made heaven and earth.

The heaven, even the heavens, are the Lord's: but the earth hath He given to the children of men.

The dead praise not the Lord, neither any that go down into silence.

But we will bless the Lord from this time forth and for evermore. Praise the Lord.

TWENTY-FIFTH DAY OF THE MONTH.

PSALM CXVI.

I love the Lord, because He hath heard my voice and my supplications.

Because He hath inclined His ear unto me, therefore will I call upon Him as long as I live.

The sorrows of death compassed me, and the pains of hell gat hold upon me: I found trouble and sorrow.

Then called I upon the name of the Lord; O Lord, I beseech Thee, deliver my soul.

Gracious is the Lord, and righteous; yea, our God is merciful.

The Lord preserveth the simple: I was brought low, and He helped me.

Return unto thy rest, O my soul; for the Lord hath dealt bountifully with thee.

For Thou hast delivered my soul from death, mine eyes from tears, and my feet from falling.

I will walk before the Lord in the land of the living.

I believed, therefore have I spoken: I was greatly afflicted:

I said in my haste, All men are liars.

What shall I render unto the Lord for all His benefits toward me?

I will take the cup of salvation, and call upon the name of the Lord.

I will pay my vows unto the Lord now in the presence of all His people.

Precious in the sight of the Lord is the death of His saints.

O Lord, truly I am Thy servant; I am Thy servant, and the son of Thine handmaid: Thou hast loosed my bonds.

I will offer to Thee the sacrifice of thanksgiving, and will call upon the name of the Lord.

I will pay my vows unto the Lord now in the presence of all His people,

In the courts of the Lord's house, in the midst of thee, O Jerusalem. Praise ye the Lord.

TWENTY-SIXTH DAY OF THE MONTH.

PSALM CXVIII.

O give thanks unto the Lord; for He is good: because His mercy endureth forever.

Let them now that fear the Lord say, that His mercy endureth forever.

I called upon the Lord in distress: the Lord answered me, and set me in a large place.

The Lord is on my side; I will not fear: what can man do unto me?

The Lord taketh my part with them that help me.

It is better to trust in the Lord than to put confidence in man.

It is better to trust in the Lord than to put confidence in princes.

The Lord is my strength and song, and is become my salvation.

The voice of rejoicing and salvation is in the tabernacles of the righteous: the right hand of the Lord doeth valiantly.

The right hand of the Lord is exalted: the right hand of the Lord doeth valiantly.

I shall not die, but live, and declare the works of the Lord.

The Lord hath chastened me sore: but He hath not given me over unto death.

Open to me the gates of righteousness: I will go into them, and I will praise the Lord:

This gate of the Lord, into which the righteous shall enter.

I will praise Thee: for Thou hast heard me, and art become my salvation.

The stone which the builders refused is become the head-stone of the corner.

This is the Lord's doing; it is marvellous in our eyes.

This is the day which the Lord hath made; we will rejoice and be glad in it.

Save now, I beseech Thee, O Lord: O Lord, I beseech Thee, send now prosperity.

Blessed be He that cometh in the name of the Lord: we have blessed you out of the house of the Lord.

God is the Lord, which hath shewed us light.

Thou art my God, and I will praise Thee: Thou art my God, I will exalt Thee.

O give thanks unto the Lord; for He is good: for His mercy endureth forever.

TWENTY-SEVENTH DAY OF THE MONTH.

PSALM CXIX.

Blessed are the undefiled in the way, who walk in the law of the Lord.

Blessed are they that keep His testimonies, and that seek Him with the whole heart.

Thou hast commanded us to keep Thy precepts diligently.

O that my ways were directed to keep Thy statutes!

Wherewithal shall a young man cleanse his way? by taking heed thereto according to Thy word.

With my whole heart have I sought Thee: O let me not wander from Thy commandments.

Thy word have I hid in mine heart, that I might not sin against Thee.

Blessed art Thou, O Lord: teach me Thy statutes.

I will delight myself in Thy statutes: I will not forget Thy word.

Deal bountifully with Thy servant, that I may live, and keep Thy word.

Open Thou mine eyes, that I may behold wondrous things out of Thy law.

I am a stranger in the earth: hide not Thy commandments from me.

Thy testimonies also are my delight and my counsellors.

Teach me, O Lord, the way of Thy statutes; and I shall keep it unto the end.

Give me understanding, and I shall keep Thy law; yea, I shall observe it with my whole heart.

Make me to go in the path of Thy commandments; for therein do I delight.

Incline my heart unto Thy testimonies, and not to covetousness.

Thou art my portion, O Lord: I have said that I would keep Thy words.

I entreated Thy favor with my whole heart: be merciful unto me according to Thy word.

I thought on my ways, and turned my feet unto Thy testimonies.

I made haste, and delayed not to keep Thy commandments.

At midnight I will rise to give thanks unto Thee because of Thy righteous judgments.

I am a companion of all them that fear Thee, and of them that keep thy precepts.

The earth, O Lord, is full of Thy mercy: teach me Thy statutes.

Thou hast dealt well with Thy servant, O Lord, according unto Thy word.

Teach me good judgment and knowledge: for I have believed Thy commandments.

Before I was afflicted I went astray: but now have I kept Thy word.

Thou art good, and doest good; teach me Thy statutes.

It is good for me that I have been afflicted; that I might learn Thy statutes.

The law of Thy mouth is better unto me than thousands of gold and silver.

Thy hands have made me and fashioned me: give

me understanding, that I may learn Thy commandments.

They that fear Thee will be glad when they see me; because I have hoped in Thy word.

I know, O Lord, that Thy judgments are right, and that Thou in faithfulness hast afflicted me.

Let, I pray Thee, Thy merciful kindness be for my comfort, according to Thy word unto Thy servant.

Let Thy tender mercies come unto me, that I may live: for Thy law is my delight.

Let my heart be sound in Thy statutes; that I be not ashamed.

TWENTY-EIGHTH DAY OF THE MONTH.

O how love I Thy law! it is my meditation all the day.

Thou through Thy commandments hast made me wiser than mine enemies: for they are ever with me.

I have more understanding than all my teachers: for Thy testimonies are my meditation.

I understand more than the ancients, because I keep Thy precepts.

How sweet are Thy words unto my taste! yea, sweeter than honey to my mouth!

Through Thy precepts I get understanding: therefore I hate every false way.

Thy word is a lamp unto my feet, and a light unto my path.

I have sworn, and I will perform it, that I will keep Thy righteous judgments.

Thy testimonies have I taken as a heritage forever: for they are the rejoicing of my heart.

I have inclined mine heart to perform Thy statutes alway, even unto the end.

I hate vain thoughts: but Thy law do I love.

Thou art my hiding-place and my shield: I hope in Thy word.

Depart from me, ye evil-doers: for I will keep the commandments of my God.

Uphold me according unto Thy word, that I may live: and let me not be ashamed of my hope.

Hold Thou me up, and I shall be safe; and I will have respect unto Thy statutes continually.

My flesh trembleth for fear of Thee; and I am afraid of Thy judgments.

Mine eyes fail for Thy salvation, and for the word of Thy righteousness.

Thy testimonies are wonderful: therefore doth my soul keep them.

The entrance of Thy words giveth light; it giveth understanding unto the simple.

Look Thou upon me, and be merciful unto me, as Thou usest to do unto those that love Thy name.

Order my steps in Thy word: and let not any iniquity have dominion over me.

Deliver me from the oppression of man: so will I keep Thy precepts.

Make Thy face to shine upon Thy servant; and teach me Thy statutes.

Rivers of waters run down mine eyes, because they keep not Thy law.

I hate and abhor lying: but Thy law do I love.

Seven times a day do I praise Thee because of Thy righteous judgments.

Lord, I have hoped for Thy salvation, and done Thy commandments.

I have kept Thy precepts and Thy testimonies: for all my ways are before Thee.

Let my supplication come before Thee: deliver me according to Thy word.

My lips shall utter praise, when Thou hast taught me Thy statutes.

My tongue shall speak of Thy word: for all Thy commandments are righteousness.

Let Thine hand help me; for I have chosen Thy precepts.

I have longed for Thy salvation, O Lord; and Thy law is my delight.

Let my soul live, and it shall praise Thee; and let Thy judgments help me.

I have gone astray like a lost sheep; seek Thy servant; for I do not forget Thy commandments.

TWENTY-NINTH DAY OF THE MONTH.

PSALM CXXXVI.

O give thanks unto the Lord; for He is good: for His mercy endureth forever.

O give thanks unto the God of gods: for His mercy endureth forever.

O give thanks to the Lord of lords: for His mercy endureth forever.

To Him who alone doeth great wonders: for His mercy endureth forever.

To Him that by wisdom made the heavens: for His mercy endureth forever.

To Him that stretched out the earth above the waters: for His mercy endureth forever.

To Him that made great lights: for His mercy endureth forever:

The sun to rule by day: for His mercy endureth forever.

The moon and stars to rule by night: for His mercy endureth forever.

Who remembered us in our low estate: for His mercy endureth forever:

And hath redeemed us from our enemies: for His mercy endureth forever.

Who giveth food to all flesh: for His mercy endureth forever.

O give thanks unto the God of heaven: for His mercy endureth forever.

PSALM CXXXIX.

O Lord, Thou hast searched me, and known me.

Thou knowest my down-sitting and mine uprising, Thou understandest my thought afar off.

For there is not a word in my tongue, but lo, O Lord, Thou knowest it altogether.

Thou hast beset me behind and before, and laid Thine hand upon me.

Such knowledge is too wonderful for me; it is high, I cannot attain unto it.

Whither shall I go from Thy Spirit? or whither shall I flee from Thy presence?

If I ascend up into heaven, Thou art there: if I make my bed in hell, behold, Thou art there.

If I take the wings of the morning, and dwell in the uttermost parts of the sea;

Even there shall Thy hand lead me, and Thy right hand shall hold me.

If I say, Surely the darkness shall cover me; even the night shall be light about me.

Yea, the darkness hideth not from Thee; but the night shineth as the day: the darkness and the light are both alike to Thee.

I will praise Thee; for I am fearfully and wonderfully made: marvellous are Thy works; and that my soul knoweth right well.

How precious also are Thy thoughts unto me, O God! how great is the sum of them!

If I should count them, they are more in number than the sand: when I awake, I am still with Thee.

Search me, O God, and know my heart: try me, and know my thoughts:

And see if there be any wicked way in me, and lead me in the way everlasting.

THIRTIETH DAY OF THE MONTH.

PSALM CXLII.

I cried unto the Lord with my voice; with my voice unto the Lord did I make my supplication.

I poured out my complaint before Him; I shewed before Him my trouble.

When my spirit was overwhelmed within me, then Thou knewest my path. In the way wherein I walked have they privily laid a snare for me.

I looked on my right hand, and beheld, but there was no man that would know me: refuge failed me; no man cared for my soul.

I cried unto Thee, O Lord: I said, Thou art my refuge and my portion in the land of the living.

Attend unto my cry; for I am brought very low: deliver me from my persecutors; for they are stronger than I.

Bring my soul out of prison, that I may praise Thy name: the righteous shall compass me about; for Thou shalt deal bountifully with me.

PSALM CXLV.

I will extol Thee, my God, O king; and I will bless Thy name forever and ever.

Every day will I bless Thee; and I will praise Thy name for ever and ever.

Great is the Lord, and greatly to be praised; and His greatness is unsearchable.

One generation shall praise Thy works to another, and shall declare Thy mighty acts.

I will speak of the glorious honor of Thy majesty, and of Thy wondrous works.

And men shall speak of the might of Thy terrible acts: and I will declare Thy greatness.

They shall abundantly utter the memory of Thy great goodness, and shall sing of Thy righteousness.

The Lord is gracious, and full of compassion; slow to anger, and of great mercy.

The Lord is good to all: and His tender mercies are over all His works.

All Thy works shall praise Thee, O Lord; and Thy saints shall bless Thee.

They shall speak of the glory of Thy kingdom, and talk of Thy power;

To make known to the sons of men His mighty acts, and the glorious majesty of His kingdom.

Thy kingdom is an everlasting kingdom, and Thy dominion endureth throughout all generations.

The Lord upholdeth all that fall, and raiseth up all those that be bowed down.

The eyes of all wait upon Thee; and Thou givest them their meat in due season.

Thou openest Thine hand, and satisfiest the desire of every living thing.

The Lord is righteous in all His ways, and holy in all His works.

The Lord is nigh unto all them that call upon Him, to all that call upon Him in truth.

He will fulfil the desire of them that fear Him: He also will hear their cry, and will save them.

The Lord preserveth all them that love Him: but all the wicked will He destroy.

My mouth shall speak the praise of the Lord and let all flesh bless His holy name forever and ever.

PSALM CXLVI.

Praise ye the Lord. Praise the Lord, O my soul.

While I live will I praise the Lord: I will sing praises unto my God while I have any being.

Put not your trust in princes, nor in the son of man, in whom there is no help.

His breath goeth forth, he returneth to his earth; in that very day his thoughts perish.

Happy is he that hath the God of Jacob for his help, whose hope is in the Lord his God:

Which made heaven, and earth, the sea, and all that therein is: which keepeth truth forever:

Which executeth judgment for the oppressed: which giveth food to the hungry. The Lord looseth the prisoners:

The Lord openeth the eyes of the blind: the Lord raiseth them that are bowed down: the Lord loveth the righteous:

The Lord preserveth the strangers; He relieveth

the fatherless and widow: but the way of the wicked He turneth upside down.

The Lord shall reign forever, even thy God, O Zion, unto all generations. Praise ye the Lord.

THIRTY-FIRST DAY OF THE MONTH.

PSALM CXLVII.

Praise ye the Lord: for it is good to sing praises unto our God; for it is pleasant; and praise is comely.

The Lord doth build up Jerusalem: He gathereth together the outcasts of Israel.

He healeth the broken in heart, and bindeth up their wounds.

He telleth the number of the stars; He calleth them all by their names.

Great is our Lord, and of great power: His understanding is infinite.

The Lord lifteth up the meek: He casteth the wicked down to the ground.

Sing unto the Lord with thanksgiving; sing praise upon the harp unto our God:

Who covereth the heaven with clouds, who prepareth rain for the earth, who maketh grass to grow upon the mountains.

He giveth to the beast his food, and to the young ravens which cry.

He delighteth not in the strength of the horse: He taketh not pleasure in the legs of a man.

The Lord taketh pleasure in them that fear Him, in those that hope in His mercy.

Praise the Lord, O Jerusalem; praise thy God, O Zion.

For He hath strengthened the bars of thy gates; He hath blessed thy children within thee.

He maketh peace in thy borders, and filleth thee with the finest of the wheat.

He sendeth forth His commandment upon earth: His word runneth very swiftly.

He giveth snow like wool: He scattereth the hoarfrost like ashes.

He casteth forth His ice like morsels: who can stand before His cold?

He sendeth out His word, and melteth them: He causeth His wind to blow, and the waters flow.

He sheweth His word unto Jacob, His statutes and His judgments unto Israel.

He hath not dealt so with any nation: and as for His judgments, they have not known them. Praise ye the Lord.

PSALM CXLVIII.

Praise ye the Lord. Praise ye the Lord from the heavens: praise Him in the heights.

Praise ye Him, all His angels: praise ye Him, all His hosts.

Praise ye Him, sun and moon: praise Him, all ye stars of light.

Praise Him, ye heaven of heavens, and ye waters that be above the heavens.

Let them praise the name of the Lord: for He commanded, and they were created.

He hath also established them forever and ever: He hath made a decree which shall not pass.

Praise the Lord from the earth, ye dragons, and all deeps:

Fire, and hail; snow, and vapors; stormy wind fulfilling His word:

Mountains, and all hills; fruitful trees, and all cedars:

Beasts, and all cattle; creeping things, and flying fowl:

Kings of the earth, and all people; princes, and all judges of the earth:

Both young men, and maidens; old men, and children:

Let them praise the name of the Lord: for His name alone is excellent; His glory is above the earth and heaven.

Selections from Other Parts of the Scriptures,

FOR AFTERNOON SERVICES, AND OTHER OCCASIONS.

FIRST SELECTION.

The Song of the Blessed Virgin.

MY soul doth magnify the Lord,
And my spirit hath rejoiced in God my Saviour.

For He hath regarded the low estate of His handmaiden: for, behold, from henceforth all generations shall call me blessed.

For He that is mighty hath done to me great things; and holy is His name.

And His mercy is on them that fear Him from generation to generation.

He hath shewed strength with His arm: He hath scattered the proud in the imagination of their hearts.

He hath put down the mighty from their seats, and exalted them of low degree.

He hath filled the hungry with good things; and the rich He hath sent empty away.

He hath holpen His servant Israel, in remembrance of His mercy;

As He spake to our fathers, to Abraham, and to His seed forever.

SECOND SELECTION.

The Song of Zacharias.

Blessed be the Lord God of Israel; for He hath visited and redeemed His people,

And hath raised up an horn of salvation for us in the house of His servant David;

As He spake by the mouth of His holy prophets, which have been since the world began;

That we should be saved from our enemies, and from the hand of all that hate us;

To perform the mercy promised to our fathers, and to remember His holy covenant,

The oath which He sware to our father Abraham;

That He would grant unto us, that we, being delivered out of the hand of our enemies, might serve Him without fear,

In holiness and righteousness before Him, all the days of our life.

And thou, child, shalt be called the Prophet of the Highest: for thou shalt go before the face of the Lord to prepare His ways;

To give knowledge of salvation unto His people, by the remission of their sins,

Through the tender mercy of our God, whereby the day-spring from on high hath visited us,

To give light to them that sit in darkness and in the shadow of death, to guide our feet in the way of peace.

THIRD SELECTION.
The Song of Moses at the Red Sea.

I will sing unto the Lord, for He hath triumphed gloriously: the horse and his rider hath He thrown into the sea.

The Lord is my strength and song, and He is become my salvation: He is my God, and I will prepare Him an habitation; my Father's God, and I will exalt Him.

The Lord is a man of war: the Lord is His name.

Pharaoh's chariots and his host hath He cast into the sea: his chosen captains also are drowned in the Red Sea.

The depths have covered them: they sank into the bottom as a stone.

Thy right hand, O Lord, is become glorious in power: Thy right hand, O Lord, hath dashed in pieces the enemy.

Who is like unto Thee, O Lord, among the gods? who is like Thee, glorious in holiness, fearful in praises, doing wonders?

Thou in Thy mercy hast led forth the people which Thou hast redeemed: Thou hast guided them in Thy strength unto Thy holy habitation.

Thou shalt bring them in, and plant them in the mountain of Thine inheritance, in the place, O Lord, which Thou hast made for Thee to dwell in; in the sanctuary, O Lord, which Thy hands have established.

Sing ye to the Lord, for He hath triumphed gloriously; the horse and his rider hath He thrown into the sea.

FOURTH SELECTION.

The Song of Moses before his Death.

Give ear, O ye heavens, and I will speak; and hear, O earth, the words of my mouth.

My doctrine shall drop as the rain, my speech shall distil as the dew; as the small rain upon the tender herb, and as the showers upon the grass:

Because I will publish the name of the Lord; ascribe ye greatness unto our God.

He is the Rock, His work is perfect; for all His ways are judgment: a God of truth, and without iniquity; just and right is He.

They have corrupted themselves; their spot is not the spot of His children: they are a perverse and crooked generation.

Do ye thus requite the Lord, O foolish people and unwise? is not He thy Father that hath bought thee? hath He not made thee, and established thee?

For the Lord's portion is His people; Jacob is the lot of His inheritance.

Of the Rock that begat thee thou art unmindful, and hast forgotten God that formed thee.

For they are a nation void of counsel, neither is there any understanding in them.

Oh that they were wise, that they understood this, that they would consider their latter end!

See now that I, even I, am He, and there is no god with me: I kill, and I make alive; I wound, and I heal: neither is there any that can deliver out of my hand.

For I lift up my hand to heaven, and say, I live forever.

Rejoice, O ye nations, with His people; for He will avenge the blood of His servants, and will render vengeance to His adversaries, and will be merciful unto His land, and to His people.

Solomon's Prayer.

Then said Solomon, The Lord hath said that He would dwell in the thick darkness.

But I have built an house of habitation for Thee, and a place for Thy dwelling forever.

(But will God in very deed dwell with men on the earth? Behold, heaven, and the heaven of heavens, cannot contain Thee; how much less this house which I have built!)

Hearken therefore unto the supplications of Thy servant, and of Thy people Israel, which they shall make toward this place: hear Thou from Thy dwelling-place, even from heaven; and when Thou hearest, forgive.

Now, my God, let, I beseech Thee, Thine eyes be open, and let Thine ears be attent unto the prayer that is made in this place.

Now therefore arise, O Lord God, into Thy resting-place, Thou, and the ark of Thy strength: let Thy priests, O Lord God, be clothed with salvation, and let Thy saints rejoice in goodness.

O Lord God, turn not away the face of Thine anointed: remember the mercies of David Thy servant.

FIFTH SELECTION.

A Song of Praise.

O Lord, Thou art my God; I will exalt Thee, I will praise Thy name; for Thou hast done wonderful things; Thy counsels of old are faithfulness and truth.

For Thou hast been a strength to the poor, a strength to the needy in his distress, a refuge from the storm, a shadow from the heat, when the blast of the terrible ones is as a storm against the wall.

And in this mountain shall the Lord of hosts make unto all people a feast of fat things, a feast of wines on the lees; of fat things full of marrow, of wines on the lees well refined.

And He will destroy in this mountain the face of the covering cast over all people, and the veil that is spread over all nations.

He will swallow up death in victory; and the Lord God will wipe away tears from off all faces; and the rebuke of His people shall He take away from off all the earth: for the Lord hath spoken it.

And it shall be said in that day, Lo, this is our God; we have waited for Him, and He will save us:

this is the Lord; we have waited for Him, we will be glad and rejoice in His salvation.

We have a strong city: salvation will God appoint for walls and bulwarks.

Open ye the gates, that the righteous nation which keepeth the truth may enter in.

Thou wilt keep him in perfect peace whose mind is stayed on Thee; because he trusteth in Thee.

Trust ye in the Lord forever: for in the Lord Jehovah is everlasting strength.

The way of the just is uprightness: Thou, most upright, dost weigh the path of the just.

Yea, in the way of Thy judgments, O Lord, have we waited for Thee; the desire of our soul is to Thy name, and to the remembrance of Thee.

With my soul have I desired Thee in the night; yea, with my spirit within me will I seek Thee early: for when Thy judgments are in the earth, the inhabitants of the world will learn righteousness.

Lord, Thou wilt ordain peace for us: for Thou also hast wrought all our works in us.

O Lord our God, other lords besides Thee have had dominion over us; but by Thee only will we make mention of Thy name.

SIXTH SELECTION.

A Triumphant Song.

I am the Lord; that is my name: and my glory will I not give to another, neither my praise to graven images.

I, even I, am the Lord; and besides me there is no Saviour.

I have blotted out, as a thick cloud, thy transgressions, and, as a cloud, thy sins: return unto me; for I have redeemed thee.

Sing unto the Lord a new song, and His praise from the end of the earth, ye that go down to the sea, and all that is therein; the isles, and the inhabitants thereof.

Let them give glory unto the Lord, and declare His praise in the islands.

Let the wilderness and the cities thereof lift up their voice, the villages that Kedar doth inhabit: let the inhabitants of the rock sing, let them shout from the top of the mountains.

Sing, O ye heavens; for the Lord hath done it: shout, ye lower parts of the earth; break forth into singing, ye mountains, O forest, and every tree therein: for the Lord hath redeemed Jacob, and glorified Himself in Israel.

Awake, awake, put on strength, O arm of the Lord; awake, as in the ancient days, in the generations of old.

Art Thou not it which hath dried the sea, the waters of the great deep; that hath made the depths of the sea a way for the ransomed to pass over?

Therefore the redeemed of the Lord shall return, and come with singing unto Zion; and everlasting joy shall be upon their head: they shall obtain gladness and joy; and sorrow and mourning shall flee away.

SEVENTH SELECTION.

A Song of Redemption.

Awake, awake; put on thy strength, O Zion; put on thy beautiful garments, O Jerusalem, the holy city.

Shake thyself from the dust; arise.

For thus saith the Lord, Ye have sold yourselves for nought; and ye shall be redeemed without money.

How beautiful upon the mountains are the feet of Him that bringeth good tidings, that publisheth peace; that bringeth good tidings of good, that publisheth salvation; that saith unto Zion, Thy God reigneth!

Thy watchmen shall lift up the voice; with the voice together shall they sing: for they shall see eye to eye, when the Lord shall bring again Zion.

Break forth into joy, sing together, ye waste places of Jerusalem: for the Lord hath comforted His people, He hath redeemed Jerusalem.

The Lord hath made bare His holy arm in the eyes of all the nations; and all the ends of the earth shall see the salvation of our God.

A Song of Rejoicing.

I will greatly rejoice in the Lord, my soul shall be joyful in my God; for He hath clothed me with garments of salvation, He hath covered me with the robe of righteousness, as a bridegroom decketh himself with ornaments, and as a bride adorneth herself with her jewels.

For as the earth bringeth forth her bud, and as the garden causeth the things that are sown in it to spring forth; so the Lord God will cause righteousness and praise to spring forth before all the nations.

A Psalm of Thanksgiving and Confession.

I will mention the loving-kindnesses of the Lord, and the praises of the Lord, according to all that the Lord hath bestowed on us, and the great goodness toward the house of Israel, which He hath bestowed on them according to His mercies, and according to the multitude of His loving-kindnesses.

For He said, Surely they are my people, children that will not lie: so He was their Saviour.

In all their affliction He was afflicted, and the angel of His presence saved them: in His love and in His pity He redeemed them; and He bare them, and carried them all the days of old.

But they rebelled, and vexed His Holy Spirit: therefore He was turned to be their enemy, and He fought against them.

Look down from heaven, and behold from the habitation of Thy holiness and of Thy glory: where is Thy zeal and Thy strength, and Thy mercies toward me? are they restrained?

Doubtless Thou art our Father, though Abraham be ignorant of us, and Israel acknowledge us not:

Thou, O Lord, art our Father, our Redeemer; Thy name is from everlasting.

O Lord, why hast Thou made us to err from Thy ways, and hardened our heart from Thy fear? Return for Thy servants' sake, the tribes of Thine inheritance.

EIGHTH SELECTION.

Oh that Thou wouldest rend the heavens, that Thou wouldest come down, that the mountains might flow down at Thy presence;

When Thou didst terrible things which we looked not for, Thou camest down, the mountains flowed down at Thy presence.

But we are all as an unclean thing, and all our righteousnesses are as filthy rags; and we all do fade as a leaf; and our iniquities, like the wind, have taken us away.

But now, O Lord, Thou art our Father: we are the clay, and Thou our potter; and we all are the work of Thy hand.

Be not wroth very sore, O Lord, neither remember iniquity forever: behold, see, we beseech Thee, we are all Thy people.

Wilt Thou refrain Thyself for these things, O Lord? wilt Thou hold Thy peace, and afflict us very sore?

Wherewith shall I come before the Lord, and bow myself before the high God? shall I come before Him with burnt-offerings, with calves of a year old?

Will the Lord be pleased with thousands of rams, or with ten thousands of rivers of oil? shall I give my first-born for my transgression, the fruit of my body for the sin of my soul?

He hath shewed thee, O man, what is good; and what doth the Lord require of thee, but to do justly, and to love mercy, and to walk humbly with thy God?

The Lord's voice crieth unto the city, and the man of wisdom shall see Thy name: hear ye the rod, and who hath appointed it.

Therefore I will look unto the Lord; I will wait for the God of my salvation: my God will hear me.

Rejoice not against me, O mine enemy; when I fall, I shall arise; when I sit in darkness, the Lord shall be a light unto me.

I will bear the indignation of the Lord, because I have sinned against Him, until He plead my cause, and execute judgment for me: He will bring me forth to the light, and I shall behold His righteousness.

Who is a God like unto Thee, that pardoneth iniquity, and passeth by the transgression of the remnant of His heritage? He retaineth not His anger forever, because He delighteth in mercy.

He will turn again, He will have compassion upon us; He will subdue our iniquities: and Thou wilt cast all their sins into the depths of the sea.

Thou wilt perform the truth to Jacob, and the mercy to Abraham, which Thou hast sworn unto our fathers from the days of old.

NINTH SELECTION.

Blessed be the name of God forever and ever: for wisdom and might are His:

And He changeth the times and the season: He removeth kings, and setteth up kings: He giveth wisdom unto the wise, and knowledge to them that know understanding:

He revealeth the deep and secret things: He knoweth what is in the darkness, and the light dwelleth with Him.

How great are His signs! and how mighty are His wonders! His kingdom is an everlasting kingdom, and His kingdom is from generation to generation.

O Lord, the great and dreadful God, keeping the covenant and mercy to them that love Him, and to them that keep His commandments;

We have sinned, and have committed iniquity, and have done wickedly, and have rebelled, even by departing from Thy precepts, and from Thy judgments:

Neither have we hearkened unto Thy servants the prophets, which spake in Thy name to our kings, our princes, and our fathers, and to all the people of the land.

O Lord, to us belongeth confusion of face, to our kings, to our princes, and to our fathers, because we have sinned against Thee.

To the Lord our God belong mercies and forgivenesses, though we have rebelled against Him.

Neither have we obeyed the voice of the Lord our God, to walk in His laws, which He set before us.

TENTH SELECTION.

We are not come unto the mount that might be touched, and that burned with fire, nor unto blackness, and darkness, and tempest,

And the sound of a trumpet, and the voice of words; which voice they that heard entreated that the word should not be spoken to them any more:

But we are come unto mount Sion, and unto the city of the living God, the heavenly Jerusalem, and to an innumerable company of angels,

To the general assembly and church of the firstborn, which are written in heaven, and to God the Judge of all and to the spirits of just men made perfect,

And to Jesus the mediator of the new covenant, and to the blood of sprinkling, that speaketh better things than that of Abel.

Holy, holy, holy, Lord God Almighty, which was, and is, and is to come.

Thou art worthy, O Lord, to receive glory, and honor, and power: for Thou hast created all things, and for Thy pleasure they are, and they were created.

Amen: Blessing, and glory, and wisdom, and thanksgiving, and honor, and power, be unto our God forever and ever.

Salvation to our God, which sitteth upon the throne, and unto the Lamb.

Unto Him that loved us and washed us from our sins in His own blood, and hath made us kings and priests unto God and His Father, to Him be glory and dominion forever. *Amen.*

A Song of Triumph.

Now is come salvation, and strength, and the kingdom of our God, and the power of His Christ: for the accuser of our brethren is cast down, which accused them before our God day and night.

And they overcame him by the blood of the Lamb, and by the word of their testimony; and they loved not their lives unto the death.

Therefore rejoice, ye heavens, and ye that dwell in them.

Great and marvellous are Thy works, Lord God Almighty; just and true are Thy ways, Thou King of saints.

Who shall not fear Thee, O Lord, and glorify Thy name? for Thou only art holy: for all nations shall come and worship before Thee; for Thy judgments are made manifest.

www.ingramcontent.com/pod-product-compliance
Lightning Source LLC
Chambersburg PA
CBHW032224230426
43666CB00033B/1215